The History and Traditions of the Pimbwe

Sarah-Jane Seel
Peter Mgawe
Monique Borgerhoff Mulder

With a Preface by
Hon. Mizengo K.P. Pinda (MP)

MKUKI NA NYOTA
DAR—ES—SALAAM

PUBLISHED BY
Mkuki na Nyota Publishers Ltd
P. O. Box 4246
Dar es Salaam, Tanzania
www.mkukinanyota.com

© Sarah-Jane Seel, Peter Mgawe and Monique Borgerhoff Mulder, 2014

ISBN 978-9987-08-286-5

Visit www.mkukinanyota.com to read more about and to purchase
any of Mkuki na Nyota books. You will also find featured authors interviews
and news about other publisher/author events. Sign up for our e-newsletters
for updates on new releases and other announcements.

Distributed worldwide outside Africa by African Books Collective.
www.africanbookscollective.com

Contents

LIST OF TABLES

LIST OF MAPS

LIST OF PICTURES

Preface

The African continent has hundreds of ethnic groups, each with different cultural traditions and languages. However our knowledge of their different histories is very limited and few have ever been recorded, let alone on paper. This is worrying because in an increasingly homogenized global culture, many of a younger generation do not know how their grandparents and great-grandparents lived. In Europe the histories of many small groups of people have been recorded for posterity. In Africa few such histories exist, and those that do are written principally by anthropologists and missionaries. The exciting thing about this book is that it is written by an Mpimbwe about the Pimbwe, a model grassroots history.

The Pimbwe are a relatively small group of people (population approximately 50,000) living in western Tanzania but are little known outside the area. They have a unique language and cultural tradition based on fishing and hunting but this is rapidly being forgotten as they rub shoulders with the outside world – through a new road network, increased trade, immigration of other people into the area, tourism and (in the future) the internet. Many youngsters are not aware of, or worse, are not even interested in how their ancestors lived.

As a Pimbwe myself, I am delighted to see that the great effort that has been made by Peter Mgawe, together with his collaborators Monique Borgerhoff Mulder and Sarah-Jane Seel, to record the history and cultural traditions of my people. Through the pages of this book I am reminded of my childhood, catching fish as they flew up the waterfalls at Lyambalyamfipa with my four pointed hook, enjoying the sparkling fresh streams and the sheltering green forests. I remember too listening to the stories of the elders around the evening fire, and watching the interactions between the Pimbwe, Rungwa, Wakwa, Gongwe, Urawila, Konongo and Fipa, all of whom live in, or regularly travel through, different parts of the Rukwa Valley.

The authors have created a fascinating document for posterity by piecing together information taken from broader historical research on East Africa that has been conducted by African and European scholars over the last century with interviews from the Pimbwe themselves. It is important to stress that this is not the history of a few Pimbwe elders with good memories for the tales of their grandparents. The history recorded here is the product of a workshop held in Mpanda in September 2008 at which men and women from all over Mpimbwe were invited to discuss their past and their identity.

We have distributed nearly 3000 copies of a shorter version of this book, Historia ya Kabila la Wapimbwe, across all the schools in Mpimbwe (now part of Katavi Region). With these two books I hope that future generations of Pimbwe will find a deeper link to their past, and to their remarkably beautiful environment. I wish too that more recent immigrants into the Rukwa Valley will enjoy this history. More broadly, I hope that this effort will inspire other young people throughout Tanzania and elsewhere in Africa to record the history of their ancestors before it is forgotten, and not rely simply on the books written by outsiders.

Mizengo P. Pinda
Prime Minister of Tanzania, July 2010

Picture 1. Workshop on the history of the Pimbwe (September 2008, Mpanda). Mizengo K.P. Pinda listening to Peter Mgawe's presentation. Photo Monique Borgerhoff Mulder.

Acknowledgements

This book is written primarily for the Pimbwe, and for others interested in the story of Mpimbwe from the pre-colonial period to the present. It is built on our own research, supplemented with secondary sources. In so doing we rely on the work of many travellers, scholars and missionaries who are cited in the bibliography, and to whom we are thankful for their meticulous chronicling of what they saw. But there are many others to whom we owe special gratitude.

First three historians: Professor Tony Waters, whose historical research in Mpanda District in part inspired this book and who made very helpful comments on the manuscript, Padre Mwiga, such an enthusiastic chronicler of both the history of the church in Rukwa and the Pimbwe language, and Professor Anselm Tambila whose thesis on the history of Rukwa Region provided such an invaluable guide. Second, we are very grateful to Tim Caro who commented on many drafts of this book, and supported numerous aspects of the research. Additionally we thank many students and collaborators: Jonathon Salerno and John Darwent for designing and researching the maps; Andimile Martin for technical and historical advice; Omari Ayubu Msago who taught us so much about the Rukwa Valley; Barnabas Caro for sharing his experiences of growing up in Mpimbwe; and all our friends in the Rukwa Valley and beyond who have helped guide us all in our research in Mpimbwe. We also give very special thanks to our dear friends Oska Ulaya and Amisa Msago, without whom life would have been very different for us in Rukwa.

This project would have been impossible without the unlimited generosity of so many men and women in Mpimbwe who talked, travelled and simply hung out with us while we tried to piece together the puzzles of their history. They were endlessly patient, gracious with their criticisms of where we had gone wrong, and often exceptionally entertaining. While we cannot name everyone who provided us with key information, we cannot fail to acknowledge the huge contributions of Daniel Kasike (*Mnyachisike*), Pascali Katagambe (*Mnyachiti*), Joseph Mapelani (*Mnyamapelani*), Melikio Mkalala, Felista Adamu (*Mkaunyese*), Desolata Kifumbe (*Mkakifumbe*), Rosalia Bululu (*Mkakusapula*), Maria Chimbachimba (*Mkakasha*), Yohana Mpepo (*Mnyamahemela*), Mnyamtubhi, Colnel Baraka, Eliasi Garimoshi (*Mnyilumba* and *Kafwagananzala*), Joseph Kazimoto, Valeli Kasamya (*Mnyasilanda*), Robert Kasogera (*Mnyakasha*), Basilio Bilia Mgawe (*Mnyamgabhe*), Valeli Kipande (*Mnyambogo*), Antoni Pigangoma (*Mnyamanyika*), Davita Gervas, Consolata Mgawe (*Mkamgabhe*), Mtemi Luchensa III (*Mnyamalaso*), Anastazia Kamangale, Bernadeta Ngomeni, Simoni Pangani Kalulu, Beata Chomba, Mzee Kafamagulu, Mzee Kanana and all the men and women who attended the workshop on the 20th September 2008. In addition, many of the village, ward and divisional leaders of Mpimbwe helped us in multiple ways.

We were also supported, in our historical work in Mpimbwe, by many able assistants, most notably Isiah Donad, Marietta Kimisha, Jenita Ponsiano, Mashaka Seni, Eliasi Uledi, and Kabi Damino. Jailos Mahenge and Joachikim Kiberinka kindly read and commented on the Kiswahili version, and various staff at the University of Dar es Salaam, together with Tony Waters, helped with archival materials. Monique and Sarah-Jane would like to thank Tim and Barnabas Caro for enormous help at the study site in Tanzania. Peter would like to acknowledge his colleagues Jofrey Mtelekela, Happiness Mhina, Komredi Massamu Yessaya and Josephati Ambilikile who discussed issues of oral history with him, as well as the constant support of his uncle, Eddiss Mgawe, his mother Jemima Ally, and his stepfather Lousi Kazembe.

Finally, we would like to thank Mheshimiwa Mizengo Pinda for the encouragement and enthusiasm he has shown for this project from its initiation, and the financial support of the Prime Minister's Office.

Sarah-Jane Seel, Peter Mgawe and Monique Borgerhoff Mulder

September 2014

Dedication

We dedicate this book to Mnya Kasike whose passion for history and razor-sharp memory inspired us all, and who passed away in March 2013; also to Peter's fathers Emanueli Mgawe and Paulo Mgawe, and his recently deceased (July 2013) brother Pantaleo Mgawe; finally to Monique and Sarah-Jane's respective parents and grandparents, René and Francoise Borgerhoff Mulder, who loved travel, adventure, and history.

Notes to Reader

Let us introduce ourselves: Monique has worked in Mpimbwe for 20 years, focusing on ecological and anthropological questions. Peter was born in Mpimbwe to Pimbwe parents and educated in the Rukwa Valley before moving away. In 2006, he joined Monique's research team as an assistant, and expressed interest in working on a history of the Pimbwe. Sarah-Jane is a graduate in History from the University of Edinburgh, and took a big role in the writing of this book after a short visit to Mpimbwe in 2011.

From this work was derived a shorter book, "Historia ya Kabila la Wapimbwe", written in Kiswahili by Peter Mgawe, Monique Borgerhoff Mulder, Tim Caro and Sarah-Jane Seel, which is distributed freely in schools in Mpimbwe, with the support of the Prime Minister's Office and the University of California at Davis. In the present book we use italics to convey Pimbwe terms (unless otherwise denoted as Kiswahili) that are either of special cultural significance to the Pimbwe or difficult to translate.

CHAPTER ONE

THE PIMBWE AND THEIR ORIGINS

1.1 Origins

There are several origin stories for the Pimbwe, revealing a difference of opinion over whether they are indigenous to the Rukwa Valley, or have more recently arrived from different locations such as Lyangalile (the southern Fipa chiefdom) or Mambwe, which lies even further to the south (see Maps 1 & 2 for the locations of identifiable place names in the text).[1]

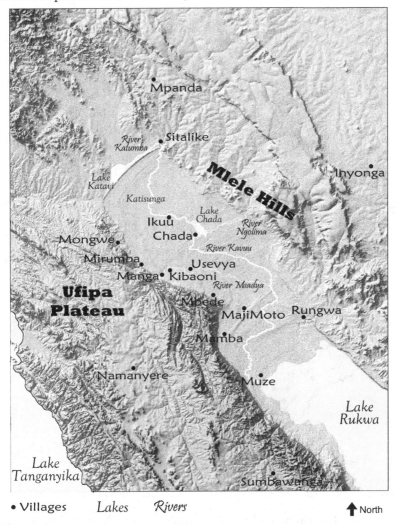

Map 1. Local map, with locations in the text identified.

1.Willis, R. The Fipa and Related Peoples of South-West Tanzania and North-East Zambia (1966), p.53. The northern Fipa chiefdom is Nkansi.

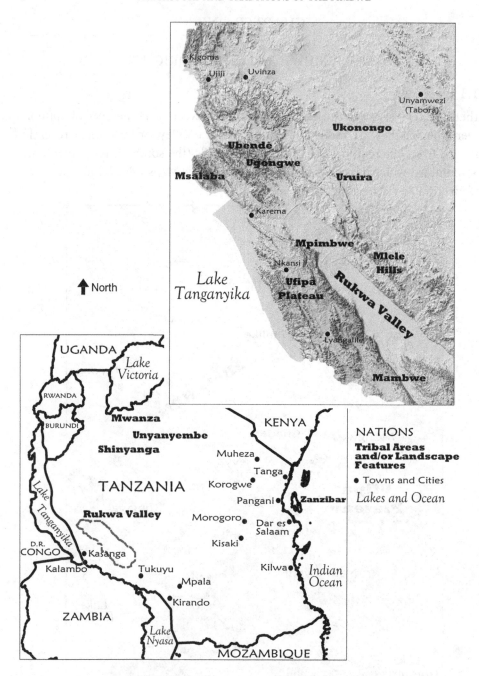

Map 2. Regional (upper right) and national maps (lower left), with locations in the text identified.

Before we explore these myths, however, we should first introduce you to the Rukwa Valley. This is part of the Great Rift that stretches from northern Syria to central Mozambique, and comprises some highly geologically active volcanic areas generating hot springs and frequent earthquakes. Archaeological investigations at

Kibaoni village show that people have probably been living in the Rukwa Valley since at least the 4th century AD. Evidence of early inhabitation comes from Early Iron Age pottery discovered in deep pits in the ground, pieces that are very similar to those found from the same period at Kalambo, which lies to the south west on the modern border with Zambia. The Rukwa Valley clearly has a long history of occupation and extensive interaction with other groups for a period of at least 1700 years.[2] Whether these early inhabitants were Pimbwe or not, in other words whether Pimbwe are indigenous to the Rukwa Valley, is a more difficult question, one with which historians still grapple.[3]

Picture 2. Archaeological excavations at the village of Kakuni (now Kibaoni) conducted in 2004. Photo Christopher O'Brien.

---

2. Foutch, A.E., et al. Faunal Analysis from Kibaoni, a Late Precolonial Pimbwe Village in Rukwa Valley, Tanzania: First Reconstructions of Cultural and Environmental Histories. Azania, 44, (2009), p.261.

3. Abe, Y. The Continuum of Languages in West Tanzania Bantu: A Case Study of Gongwe, Bende and Pimbwe. In Geographical Typology and Linguist Areas, edited by O. Hieda, C. König and H. Nakagawa. 2011.

The evidence for the Pimbwe being indigenous to the Rukwa Valley is based on a mixture of written evidence and Pimbwe elders' stories that suggest the Pimbwe established itself long ago as a small ethnic group with its own independent rulers, distinct from other groups. It was not under the rule of Fipa nor Nyamwezi, and predated the famous stories, told below, of hunters coming from these areas. In other words, the Pimbwe have their origins in the Mpimbwe territory, and call themselves the Pimbwe people.

The alternative view, also based on the stories of elders and the reports of missionaries and anthropologists, holds that the Pimbwe are immigrants to the Rukwa Valley. There are four different migration stories which combine various elements, but all of which involve hunting, a dog, water (usually hot), fraternal conflict and the legitimacy conferred by sleeping on the ground. All are based on the premise that the discovery and settlement of the Pimbwe area began as a result of the availability of water and animals.

Both Pimbwe elders and Roy Willis, the first professional anthropologist to work in Rukwa, tell of a similar story. Two young cousins (or perhaps uncle and nephew), Luchensa and Chondo, went out hunting in the Lyangalile area of Ufipa and successfully killed an animal but could not find any water to drink. Their hunting dog ran away. When he reappeared covered in mud they knew there was water nearby. Luchensa followed the dog, who led him to a hot water spring. The cousins interpreted the appearance of water under this rock as the work of spirits, and named the place "*Palichindi*" (Kipimbwe), meaning "a place of wonders". By now, night was approaching so they prepared a sleeping place. Luchensa, the younger of the two, slept on the ground whilst Chondo slept in the bed of sticks that he had made. In the morning, a conflict arose over who should become chief of the new land. Chondo claimed he deserved to be the Chief because he was older, whilst Luchensa argued that he deserved the honour since he had already slept on the land. After much debate, they returned home for their elders to resolve the problem. The elders prescribed that the land should go to the dog because it had discovered the spring. The place thereafter became known as Mpinimbwa, meaning "give it to the dog" (*mbwa* means dog in Kipimbwe). Since the dog could not rule, Luchensa was named chief because he had slept on the land. When the missionaries arrived, they mispronounced Mpinimbwa and the area became known as Mpimbwe. Chondo was to succeed Luchensa, becoming the second chief.

Picture 3. Luchensa and his dog (Origins story re-enacted, 2010). Photo Aditya Swami.

Some disagreement exists over the origins of Luchensa and Chondo. One prevailing story is that the Pimbwe came from western Africa and, after crossing the area now known as the Democratic Republic of Congo and Lake Tanganyika, started to search for a place to settle.[4] They made their traditional leader, Mwami Mwakanakusima, their chief in this mission. The Pimbwe passed along the lake coast, through the Bendeni hills at Ubende and on through Uruira, until they reached a place known as Itetemya (believed to lie somewhere to the north east of Lake Rukwa) where they established their first settlements. The children of Mwakanakusima, Chondo and Luchensa, subsequently discovered water in a new area (the story described above) and established a new chiefdom, calling it Mpimbwe. This was seen as a suitable area in which to settle because it had water, animals and honey, all of which were essential to founding a settlement. It is also said that the two daughters of Mwakanakusima, Namkale and Mwasi, went on to establish their chiefdom in Rungwa, to the east of Itetemya. The importance of the chief's mother in Fipa-related peoples (further expanded below) suggests that women may have been important in the transmission of ethnic identity and status.

Another explanation advanced by both the anthropologist Roy Willis and missionaries was that the point of origin was at a village allegedly somewhere in southern Ufipa called Kawe. Kawe is also known as Mwakanakusima which

---

4. Oral interview with Professor Anselm Tambila, University of Dar es Salaam (June 2011).

means "a fearless person" and is also the name of the woman described above. This leader, her children, and her followers set out from Kawe in search of a new home.[5] They reached Lyangalile and settled there for a short period. They then crossed the Rukwa Valley, passed Itetemya and continued to Ukonongo to the east of today's Upimbwe where Luchensa married the daughter of an old chief. The chief gave them land so that they could be self-sufficient, and Syambwe, one of Luchensa's followers, was selected to be governor of the area.[6] One day, when the small group had moved back into what was to become the Pimbwe area, Luchensa and Chondo went out hunting to find some meat as Luchensa was holding a big celebration at his home. This expedition of course was to herald Luchensa becoming chief owing to the discovery of a hot water spring, now known as Maji Moto (Kiswahili for "hot water") but originally called Pimbwe village.[7]

A final perspective on the Pimbwe's founding came from the oldest surviving member of the community, Daniel Kasike.[8] According to this version, the old name of Mpimbwe was Itaba. Itaba was a territory of a place called Ibanda, previously part of Lyangalile. According to this story, the original inhabitants of the Rukwa Valley were a sub-group of the Fipa who were, at least temporarily, integrated into the lands of the Lyangalile fiefdom (the divisions and alliances within the Fipa at this time would give credence to this story). When Luchensa and Chondo went on their hunting expedition, this was a new settlement in a previously inhabited (and possibly still inhabited) valley. The name then became Upimbwe.

1.2 Pimbwe Before the Coming of Foreigners

Upimbwe[9] is one of several small chiefdoms in the north of the Rukwa Valley sharing common boundaries with the Fipa, Bende, Gongwe, Konongo, and Rungwa. Some mid-20th century anthropologists such as Roy Willis emphasise communal values inherent in village communities in the previous century, and a strongly ethnically cohesive unit.[10] More recently, historians have questioned the existence of discrete tribal groups. For example, John Iliffe, makes the point that, "early nineteenth century Tanganyika was not inhabited by discrete compact, and identifiable tribes, each with a distinct territory, language, culture,

---

5. The fact that Kawe is associated with the origins of the Pimbwe helps explain why they refer to their ruling line as Abantu ya Kawe, meaning "children of Kawe." A daughter of "Kawe" is given the title Nyina Mwene and her male children are eligible for the chiefship.

6. Willis (1966), p.54.

7. Père Maurice. La Géographie LXIV, Les Pays des Bapimbwe (1935), p.241.

8. Oral interview with Daniel Kasike (July 2011).

9. To clarify the terminology, Upimbwe refers to the location of the traditional chieftainship, Wapimbwe to the people of the area (singular Mpimbwe), Kipimbwe to the language, and Mpimbwe to the modern administrative designation. In ambiguous context, the simple term "Pimbwe" is used.

10. Willis (1966), p.xi.

and political system", explaining that, although "the use of such collective names [is] inescapable, ... they distort and oversimplify a vastly more complex reality."[11] This is corroborated by Anselm Tambila, who notes that there were many cases in which members of ethnic groups moved around the region settling in different territories, therefore making any attempts at "compartmentalization" of the tribes futile.[12] He goes on to say that small chieftainships like the Pimbwe were able to absorb newcomers, and this prevented them from becoming extinguished. Furthermore, as we will see later in this book, there were many internal dissensions among the Pimbwe, as among other ethnic units.

Willis' emphasis on communal values is nevertheless consistent with the stories of Pimbwe elders who insist that multiple families living in the same neighbourhood cooked together and ate from the same pot, as well as the fact that African village communities and ethnic groups are – to this day – much stronger cohesive units than most communities in the developed world. However, as we will see in the upcoming chapters, Pimbwe communities have most likely always been characterized by both intra and intercommunity conflict, and became deeply entwined in the social dynamism of mid-19th century rural East Africa.

The Pimbwe country was ruled by a chief (*Mwene*) in association with his mother, known as the queen-mother (*Wacisongwa*) who was also a very important person. The chiefs of Pimbwe succeeded matrilineally. This meant that the son of the chief's sister (*Mwipwa*) was the one given the rights of being elected as a successor, a tradition which remains today. Every woman born of a womb of the royal line (*Abantu ya Kawe*, meaning "children of Kawe") was given the title Nyina Mwene, and her male children were eligible for inheriting the chiefship.[13] The country was divided into administrative districts (*ivikandawa*), each of which was under the authority of a sub-chief called *Mwene Nkandawa*. The villagers then elected village chiefs or headmen (*Basengi*), and nominations were supposed to be confirmed by the *Mwene*.[14] Chiefs did not have an elaborate court; elders were supposed to keep them in check and help with the affairs of state.

Traditionally, the Pimbwe subsisted on horticulture, small animal herding, hunting and fishing. Their crops included millet and cassava and, after its introduction, maize. Unusually for the region, the Pimbwe did not grow beans due to either a shortage of moisture and/or the fact that game and domestic meat

11. Iliffe, J. A Modern History of Tanganyika. Cambridge: Cambridge University Press (1979), p.8.

12. Tambila, A. A History of Rukwa Region (Tanzania) ca. 1870-1940: Aspects of Economic and Social Change from Pre-Colonial to Colonial Times. Ph.D. diss., University of Hamburg (1981), p.16.

13. Willis (1966), p.55.

14. Willis (1966), p.55.

were a preferred source of protein. Tribute in the form of labour and goods were critical to the power base of the chiefs, and made them wealthy. They would, for example, be given some meat or fish from hunting or fishing expeditions, and in return, citizens were provided with physical and social security.[15] Tambila stresses the importance of the production of goods in agriculture and small-scale industry at this time, in introducing the developments of the 19th century into the area. He notes that "it can only be from production that one can start engaging in trade,"[16] and that – even before the arrival of foreigners – the inhabitants of Rukwa had been involved in regional trade.[17] Local trade networks were therefore not the invention of Arabs and Swahili Muslims coming from the Indian Ocean coast, Zanzibar, Muscat or Oman, but instead a home-grown product resulting from local enterprise as will be discussed below.

Picture 4. The remains of a traditional round Pimbwe house believed to have been part of the chief's compound in Maji Moto. Photo Monique Borgerhoff Mulder (2009).

In pre-colonial times, work on the fields was organized on a family basis. Agricultural goods were produced on peoples' own land and on that of their rulers. Large families were an asset, not just to help in the fields, but also to act as insurance in old age.[18] A system of cultivation known as *miande* was used by the Pimbwe and

---

15. Tambila (1981), p.60.

16. Tambila (1981), p.7.

17. Tambila (1981), p.16.

18. Tambila (1981), p.27.

other surrounding ethnic groups. The process involved cutting down the grass with a hoe, digging up the soil and covering the grass with soil, and then planting the seeds in lines of ridges.[19] This was combined with intercropping, and with alternate cropping between the years, allowing for continued fertility of the soil for up to twelve years. This method obviated the need for constant movement of peoples.

Some sources report that the dominant mode of labour mobilization at this time was communal, in the sense that a whole village was involved in activities such as digging and harvesting. Such bands of collective labourers would move from homestead to homestead until all the fields were harvested. Rewards came in kind with either a big meal (such as chicken or goat) or a beer party. Such communal involvement was also important for other modes of production such as fishing, cloth making and hunting. In the latter case, mutual assistance was imperative for success; this is because each member brought his own length of net which was then combined to form a long net that, according to explorer Edward Hore, stretched "about half a mile in length and six feet high."[20] Animals would be chased in the direction of the net to be caught and speared, with each person involved receiving something from the victory. Another item produced at this time was iron which the Bantu people had brought to East Africa almost two thousand years earlier. It was a specialist occupation involving a high degree of technical advancement (this explains why the smelters were often referred to as *Mwene*, meaning "King").

Other important commodities made in pre-colonial times which were incorporated into local and regional trade were honey, salt, palm oil, fish, forged iron, ivory, cloth, baskets, and copper. Elephant hunting, together with the production of honey and beeswax, were the most important specialist activities, and had their origins long before the arrival of foreigners, though ivory subsequently enticed outsiders to trade in remote areas like Rukwa. Cloth making was not a specialized activity, and relied on communal village labour; cloth was often then exchanged for other commodities such as food, iron tools, pots or baskets. Explorers who travelled through the Fipa Plateau in the 1860s describe the abundant growth of cotton. For example, David Livingstone remarked in his "Last Journals" that "Much cloth was made in these parts before the Mazitu [Ngoni] raids began, it was striped black and white, and many shawls are seen in the country yet."[21]

---

19. Oral interview with Victor Kalelembe (July 2011).

20. Lechaptois, A. Aux Rives du Tanganyika. Maison Caree, Algiers (1932), p.262; Tambila (1981), p.28.

21. Willis (1966), p.xiii.

The Rukwa Valley was also famous for the production of salt, although not in the areas inhabited by the Pimbwe.[22] It became one of the most highly prized household commodity and trade goods – it was a sign of wealth and well-being to put a lot of salt in food. Its importance can be seen in the fact that, although only produced in a couple of areas, it found its way into the far corners of the Rukwa Valley. Furthermore, salt trade routes were exploited as a means of transport for other goods once the colonists arrived. Père Maurice, a Catholic Father living in Rukwa during the early part of the 20th century, notes, however, that not everyone could get access to the particularly high quality salt from Uvinza, and reports the harvesting of salty plants from the plains around Pimbwe village (now Maji Moto); these are burnt, and the ash added directly to the cooking pot.[23]

In spite of difficulties arising from the Ngoni raids (which will be discussed below), natural disasters and famines, it is likely the pre-colonial era (i.e. before about 1840) was a time when productivity, some prosperity and civility prevailed in Mpimbwe. For example, the geographer and explorer Joseph Thomson reveals in a report he made whilst travelling through the territory of the Fipa in 1880 that there is "no more peaceful race in all central Africa; they are more purely agricultural race than any other tribe I have seen. To the cultivation of their fields, they devote themselves entirely."[24,25] To what extent this characterizes Mpimbwe we cannot know, although our other historical sources make no mention of warfare. Many historians like to emphasise how violent the mid to late 19th century was, and there is without question a considerable degree of truth in this. Not all areas were consistently ravaged by war and disease, and Mpimbwe appears to have been somewhat spared, for much of the century. Nevertheless, peace and prosperity (to the extent they reigned in this part of Eastern Africa) were soon to be entirely disrupted, replaced by a climate of fear and chaos resulting from the slave trade. This triggered an ecological crisis bringing disease and famine, and the imposition of foreign rule with its accompanying military expeditions.

---

22. Plentiful sources of salt were found in Uvinza along the Malaagrasi river some 200 kms north of Pimbwe. A less significant amount was also found at Ivuna in the Rukwa Valley.

23. Père Maurice, La Géographie LXVII, Les Pays des Bapimbwe (1937), p.160.

24. Thomson, J. To the Central African Lakes and Back, Vol II (1881, reprinted 1968), p.217; Tambila (1981), p.23.

25. Willis, R. The Peace Puzzle in Ufipa. In Societies at Peace: Anthropological Perspectives, edited by S. Howell and R. Willis. London: Routledge (1989)

CHAPTER TWO

OUTSIDERS COME TO MPIMBWE

2.1 The Ngoni Raids

One of the first forces to interfere with the endogenous development of Rukwa was the arrival of the Ngoni warriors. This, the historian Tony Waters argues, "set the stage for an extremely violent 19th century."[26] Although the Ngoni are typically described as a group (known as Jere from northern Zululand) fleeing from the threat of domination by the Zulu emperor Shaka,[27] it seems clear they most likely had origins in other places as well. Juhani Koponen, an ecological historian, cites estimates that at the beginning of colonialism, only a few hundred of the 16,000-20,000 Ngoni in the Tanzanian area had Southern African origins.[28] Much of this army comprised of war prisoners, slaves, adventurers and other disaffected elements. They adopted the military style of short stabbing spears and big shields of cow skin, and fought in pincer movement formations of 200-300 men. Also known as Watuta, the first Ngoni groups crossed the Zambezi in 1825 and entered the Rukwa Valley in the early 1840s. Koponen explains how, after having created two separate kingdoms, Mshope in the north, and Njelu in the south, they conducted raids hundreds of kilometres away from their base, capturing many women and children,

"The main group rolled on like a snowball and grew fat by incorporating new members, mainly women and children from the conquered peoples."[29]

They deposed the chiefs of the Fipa Plateau, taking all available cattle back with them to what is probably now modern Malawi.[30] Adolphe Lechaptois, a missionary bishop serving in the Tanzanian Catholic dioceses of Karema, Kigoma, Mpanda and Mbeya for twenty-six years starting in 1872, reports conversations with old men in Ufipa who were children at the time of the Ngoni conquest and recalled a desperate scene,

"[The Ngoni] stayed in Ufipa for six or seven years ... After having ravaged the country, destroying many villages and massacring thousands of people, they were forced to begin cultivating food for themselves, and to spare the rest of the

26. Waters, T. Social Organisation and Social Status in 19th and 20th Century Rukwa, Tanzania, African Studies Quarterly ,Vol. 11, (2009), p.64.

27. Willis, R. A State in the Making: Myth, History and Social Transformation in Pre-Colonial Ufipa (1981), p.78.

28. Koponen, J. People and Production in late Pre-Colonial Tanzania: History and Structures, Helsinki: Finnish Society of Development Studies (1988), p.77.

29. Koponen (1988), p.77.

30. Willis (1981) p.78-79; Waters (2009), p.64.

population."[31]

It is likely that the Ngoni remained in the area until a succession dispute arose after the death of one of the leading commanders, Zwangendaba. This resulted in the opposing factions splitting up and leaving the area in different directions. It was not until the 1850s that the Ngoni attacked the Rukwa Valley again. In 1858, the English explorer Richard Burton travelled through Tabora and northern Rukwa, and described the route as "a howling wilderness, once populous and fertile, but now laid waste by the fierce [Ngoni]."[32]

There is no doubt that the Ngoni inspired terror wherever they went.[33] They were most likely assisted in their raids by the expansion of external trade and slave raiding at this time which contributed to a climate of economic and social instability, and population displacement, that the Ngoni could turn to their advantage.[34] There was, nevertheless, a positive consequence of the Ngoni raids. The indigenous groups in the Fipa area became pro-active in two ways: firstly, in building a military system which could act as both defence and attack (possibly the origins of the *ruga-ruga*[35] army, to be discussed later), and secondly in constructing palisaded fortresses around chiefdoms to guard against any future pillaging.[36] In short, the Ngoni occupation helped to stimulate a process of political and administrative centralization. This development, not entirely surprisingly, coincided with the opening up of Rukwa to trade in slaves, ivory and manufactured commodities, to which we now turn.

2.2 The Extension of Trade Routes and the Slave Trade

The mid-19th century heralded the start of the era of East and Central African exploration. Whilst the Nyamwezi (who lived around Tabora) had acted as mediators in trading ivory from the interior with the Zanzibari merchants (Arab and Swahili) of the east coast from around 1800, there were most likely few serious slaving expeditions into Rukwa before the Ngoni invasions.[37] However, over the next few decades, the societies of the Rukwa Valley were to witness a dramatic transformation, largely owing to their significant involvement in the escalating

---

31. Lechaptois (1932), p.56; Willis (1981), p.78.

32. Waters (2009), p.64.

33. Iliffe (1979), p.55.

34. Koponen (1988), p.80.

35. All the war leaders to emerge in this region retained ruga-ruga; they were a body of freelance warriors who consisted of war captives, deserters, runaway slaves and adventurers. They were trained to be personal soldiers of the chiefs who insisted upon total allegiance. Willis (1981), p.92; Waters (2009), p.61-62.

36. Willis (1981), p.80; Shorter, A. Chiefship in Western Tanzania (1972), p.276.

37. Willis (1981), p.82.

trade in slaves, ivory, firearms, and other commodities.

This transformation saw the 'opening up' of the western interior along with its incorporation into the emerging world market through long-distance trade across the Indian Ocean.[38] The Pimbwe had important trade goods, in particular the ivory that was abundant in the Rukwa Valley and in strong demand with Arab traders.[39] The high elephant density in the Rukwa Valley, coupled with rising ivory prices in Zanzibar, precipitated a strong Zanzibari Arab presence in the region.[40] It says something of the value of this resource that the Pimbwe were also prepared to organize caravans to go to Tabora market, the major inland centre of transcontinental trade at this time, to sell ivory.

Rukwa became incorporated into the wider world through trade in commodities other than ivory; namely cotton, cloth, guns, gunpowder, rubber and slaves. Furthermore, caravans crossing the territory required food for their slaves and porters which led to the sale of basic provisions and food stuffs. Cloth was also in high demand, but local production was handcrafted which meant it was in short supply amongst a growing population.[41] Many local traders at this time therefore preferred to be paid in cloth rather than money, leading to an increase in imports from Europe[42] and a consolidation of the cloth frontier. The increased supply of guns and gunpowder was to become another marked feature of the second half of the 19th century. Fulfilling a large demand for use in hunting expeditions, as well as for war and self-defence, the chiefs in Rukwa traded ivory for guns. Indeed, it is estimated that between the 1840s and the 1880s, the total number of guns transported from Zanzibar to the mainland rose from 5,000 to 100,000.[43]

The arrival of Arab traders in the region created a different status group in Rukwa, whose primary concern was facilitation of the ivory trade and safe traverse of caravans back across central Africa to the Indian Ocean.[44] Zanzibari Arabs became semi-permanent hunters and traders in the region, but initially without the power to threaten chiefly rule. Whilst the Arabs claimed to bring civilization to the comparatively underdeveloped interior, they also recognized their vulnerabilities and tended to rely on relations with African rulers to bolster their positions. For instance Chief Kapuufi of Nkansi, the Fipa chieftaincy to the

---

38. Koponen (1988), p.53.

39. Koponen tells us that ivory was used for keys, piano keys and luxury goods such as bangles. Koponen (1988), p.58.

40. By the turn of the 19th century, Zanzibar had become an important trading centre, attracting individual traders and merchant houses from the Arabian Peninsula, India, Britain, France, Germany and the USA. Tambila (1981), p.67. Ivory prices apparently increased six fold between the 1820s and the 1890s there. Iliffe (1979), p.40.

41. Père Maurice (1937), p.233.

42. Tambila (1981), p.75, 78. The cloth originally came from America but was made into seketa cloth in Europe.

43. Iliffe (1979), p.51.

44. Waters (2009), p.65.

west of Mpimbwe, had an Arab 'prime minister' in the early 1880s, an indication of how Arabs became involved with governance in Rukwa.[45]

By the late 1850s, Tanzania's elephants were rapidly disappearing, and yet the demand for ivory persisted, driving up its price. In response, Arab hunters began to advance the ivory frontier beyond Lake Tanganyika and the Rukwa Valley into the Congo, which still had an abundance of elephants. The effect of this movement was to change the dynamics of the trading system, and also to encourage the growth of slavery and the slave trade which was associated with the demands of the caravan system of transport.[46] In a process that Tambila describes as 'mercantilist capitalism', slaves were needed as ivory carriers across central Tanzania to the coast. The caravans moved between depots/fortresses in Uvinza and Tabora, while guarding the wealth-bearing caravans from attack and against the escape of slaves. There was also increasing demand for labour to work on the newly established clove and coconut plantations on the coast, in the rice fields of the interior, or even as domestics on Nguja island in Zanzibar.[47] By the 1880s, it had become more lucrative to sell slaves within Tanzania than to export them.[48]

There is some debate about the extent of the ravages of the slave trade in Rukwa during this period. Tambila denies that there was significant slaving there[49] (which was confirmed in oral accounts collected in Pimbwe in 2011) whilst Iliffe says that Arabs rarely engaged in slave raiding in Rukwa (but were nevertheless willing to purchase slaves – which of course boosts the slaving industry). It seems most likely that merchants in the area became increasingly involved in the slave trade following the significant depletion of ivory, replacing ivory with human beings in their quest for guns and gunpowder, cotton and beads. Indeed, there is considerable evidence that slavery in the inter-lacustrine region between Lake Tanganyika and Lake Rukwa had to some extent replaced ivory as the region's foremost trade by the 1870s.[50]

2.3 The Effects of Long Distance Trade

The growth of long distance trade in many goods, but particularly slaves and ivory, heralded Rukwa's integration into a commercial sphere stretching as far as India, Europe and North America.[51] This created a climate of violence and uncertainty in which some people reaped great benefits, whilst others suffered sorely. Indeed

45. Waters (2009), p.63; Iliffe (1979), p.51.

46. Iliffez (1979), p.49.

47. Tambila (1981), p.47.

48. Tambila (1981), p.50.

49. Tambila (1981), p.76.

50. Iliffe (1979), p.47, 50.

51. Tambila (1981), p.87.

those who were neither wealthy nor well-connected found themselves threatened by attack and death. H.H. Johnston, a British explorer and scholar who was later to become an important colonial administrator, provides evidence of this. His description of the carnage and devastation that he encountered on his visit to the plateau between Lakes Nyasa and Tanganyika in 1889-1890 is indicative of what was occurring across so many areas of Rukwa at this time,

> "I … have seen all human life and culture stamped out for a distance of 50 miles along the road, where only a short time before the most flourishing villages existed, surrounded by thriving crops, and enriched with abundant supplies of stored grain."[52]

This extension of trading opportunities gave already powerful chiefs, such as we have already met in Upimbwe, the chance to strengthen their state systems and become even more influential. It also stimulated the emergence of *ruga-ruga*, informally organized bands of fighters, who will play such an important role in the story we are to tell. Material aggrandizement and territorial expansion were always the chiefs' top priority and, with the backing of their *ruga-ruga*, these chiefs became, "violent and charismatic figures…[each one seeking] an advantage in the newly arrived world markets of ivory and slaves."[53] The chiefs' quests for trade items contributed to a large part of their wealth. This wealth was supplemented by the tribute, which chiefs exacted from their subordinates, as well as the custom and transit dues paid by passing caravans. Recognising the value of trade the chiefs began also to participate personally in trading expeditions to Tabora or the coast, a strategy which avoided the inclusion of middlemen and therefore enabled them to acquire net profits.[54] The chiefs' constant appetite for wealth and status meant that they were often ruthless and scheming in their activities, often suppressing their subordinates and the peasants. The differing lifestyle between the powerful and the powerless demonstrates the ever-growing distance between rulers and citizens at this time. This division is neatly summed up by Waters who writes of the emergence of "a strong separation between common people and powerful rulers…even though they may have spoken the same language and had the same "tribal affiliation."[55]

However, life was not always easy for rulers and they certainly encountered difficulties at this time. More specifically the growth of powerful incoming Arabs in the area was a problem for local chiefs, challenging their economic hegemony. Although the Arabs were initially too weak to significantly disrupt the political structures in the region, once the elephant herds had been largely destroyed and

---

52. Willis (1966), p.xiv.

53. Waters (2009) p.57.

54. Tambila (1981), p.75.

55. Tambila (1981), p.57.

chiefly power was in concomitant decline, "the traders were more willing to fight and dominate Africans."[56] These new merchant warlords built up their own armies of thugs, again referred to as *ruga-ruga*, and became threatening sources of power in their own right, intervening in succession quarrels and attacking and deposing local African leaders. Most notably the infamous Swahili Arab elephant hunters Matumula who was briefly based in Karema, and the more widely known Tippu Tip,[57] caused much social upheaval, focusing their line of attack on vulnerable smaller states such as Upimbwe.[58] Matumula, for instance, managed to assert sovereignty over, and send his *ruga-ruga* to demand tribute from, large parts of Unyamwezi, completely circumventing the powerful Nyamwezi chief Mirambo, who was himself dubbed – rightly or wrongly - as an "African Napoleon";[59] furthermore through conniving with the recently-arrived Belgian International African Association (IAA) Matumula acquired a foothold on the eastern side of Lake Tanganyika.[60] In the face of such merchant ambition, the tribal chiefs of the area formed enemies and alliances both amongst themselves and with foreign intruders in an attempt to protect their wealth, status and territory. It was this climate of instability that led to a period known as the "Small Wars", taking place between 1860 and 1898.

One major point of rivalry during the "Small Wars" was between the Pimbwe chiefs Mfundo and Kasogera. Both allied themselves with different neighbouring chiefs, the former with chief Mirambo of the Nyamwezi, and the latter with chief Kimalaunga of the Fipa, in their battle for the control of Mpimbwe. Mfundo quickly became unpopular because he was a poor administrator and a cruel man. He killed many people who did not support him, for example, he had his arch enemy Lumaliza assassinated; Lumaliza was a threat to Mfundo's position because he was seen by elders as a potential successor. There are also unverified reports that Mfundo killed the queen-mother, Mwasi Kankoma. As a result of Mfundo's unpopularity, Kasogera began to reassert control of Upimbwe, but was impeded by the common belief that he did not belong to the legitimate chiefly family line.

Mfundo did not withdraw from politics. In 1880, Mfundo was assisted by the

---

56. Iliffe (1979), p.48.

57. Tippu Tip, otherwise known as Hamed bin Hamed, was a renowned caravaneer, slave trader, elephant hunter and empire builder of the 19th century. His caravans were financed by the wealthiest and most influential Indian of the era, Sir Taria Topan. See Farrant, L. Tippu Tip and the East African Slave Trade (1975).

58. Tambila (1981), p.83.

59. Mirambo was considered to be the most famous empire builder of the region from the 1860s until his death in 1884. Not only did he pose a threat to the Zanzibaris trading route from Tabora to Ujiji (on Lake Tanganyika), but he also stirred up difficulties for them in Tabora itself. Willis (1981), p.92. Mirambo was referred to by the Germans as the African Napoleon. Père Maurice (1935), p.241.

60. In fact, this Belgian relationship turned out to be to the detriment of Matumula since the Belgians gave Karema over to the White Fathers missionaries in 1885. This did not lead to a fruitful rapport and many skirmishes ensued (Tambila, 1981, p.86).

Nyamwezi chief Mirambo and his ally Chief Simba[61] in their invasion of the Fipa and Pimbwe territories, a treacherous act. Mfundo and Mirambo attacked the Kasogera chiefly compound; Kasogera was injured on his stomach by a spear, and his sisters and sons were taken into captivity in Urambo. With the help of the *ruga-ruga*, Mfundo won the war and Kasogera's forces retreated.

Strangely, some Englishmen became involved in this turmoil. The Belgian King Leopold's IAA were starting to prospect in the area and had sent four Indian elephants via Karema for use in the eastern Congo territories. Since three of the elephants died by the time they reached Lake Tanganyika, the mission was aborted and two Englishmen employed under King Leopold, named Carter and Cadenhead, turned back for the East African coast. They decided to take a southerly route to passing through Tabora, but unfortunately became caught up in the heavy fighting that took place in Pimbwe, just as Mirambo and Mfundo were jointly attacking the Kasogera compound. Carter and Cadenhead were killed during the fighting.

Mfundo did not enjoy much of a victory over Kasogera. His *ruga-ruga* were keen to return to Unyanyembe and - without any troops to defend him - Mfundo realized he could not become chief. Despite victory, he therefore ceded power back to Kasogera. Kasogera proceeded to kill some of his potential challengers, who were still questioning his chiefly credentials. Kasogera's death in the 1880s resulted in a succession crisis since he had eliminated all prospective claimants.[62]

During this period of the "Small Wars" the Pimbwe were also attacked by their neighbours, the Gongwe and Konongo, leading to more deaths and disturbances. One particularly violent attack resulted in the death of Kasogera's mother: elders say that Gongwe hunters skinned her alive and impaled her on a post.[63] Violence in this period was exacerbated by the arrival of guns in the region which, as recounted earlier, came from Western Europe and North America in conjunction with the slaving and ivory trade. Guns were used not just for hunting purposes but also for self-defence. Although their accuracy was questionable, their use meant that fighting took on a different dimension, resulting in much more serious war wounds. Guns may also have guaranteed a larger supply of meat which may have been partly responsible for a slight increase in the population in the mid 19th century. However, population growth was short-lived and probably lasted only a few decades.[64]

---

61. Chief Simba had apparently allied with Mfundo and Mirambo to invade the Fipa and Pimbwe lands back in 1880, but he is a shadowy figure. Contemporary accounts by explorers describe him and his followers being associated with Ukonongo (Waters, 2009, p.66). Questions about his status in local history were met with puzzlement from Pimbwe and Konongo informants.

62. Waters (2009), p.66, 85.

63. Waters (2009), p.66.

64. Waters (2009), p.77.

In these times of violence and shifting alliances, chiefdoms like Mpimbwe recognized the urgent need to regroup and structure themselves differently in order to stave off attacks, both from neighbouring local chiefs and intrusive hunters hungry for ivory. Fortified villages became increasingly common, consisting of dry moats and wooden palisades.[65] Along with protecting the power of the chief, privileged residents including the queen-mother, the chief sorcerer, administrative chief, the chief's wives, and the *ruga-ruga* were kept safe inside. These fortified villages allowed chiefs to protect their ivory wealth, and provided refuge for loyal vassals to retreat in the event of an attack.[66] Farming communities often abandoned their exposed peripheral dwellings to cluster nearer to these palisaded villages. These fortified villages lasted just a few decades before native raiders or ambitious foreigners overran them but there is no doubt that they dominated social organization during the late 19th and early 20th century in Rukwa.

Long distance trade brought not only the "Small Wars" but also cheap European and American goods such as oil palm, rubber, tobacco, pottery and cloth. These goods flooded the market, and stifled demand for locally manufactured products. In 1889 the missionary-explorer Edward Hore voiced his sadness over the decline of small-scale local artisanship around the shores of Lake Tanganyika,

> *"In view of large commercial undertakings, involving ... import of manufactures, there is scarcely a temptation for enterprise. It is to be regretted that the sudden flooding of some regions of Africa with cheap European goods has simply obliterated many valuable native industries which, under careful encouragement, might have been more profitably preserved."[67]*

The resulting disengagement of the region's workers left many of them searching for employment from foreigners and resulted in some turning to porterage or slavery. However, the number who became porters was tempered by the fact that Rukwa was neither at the start nor finish of caravan sojourns until after the 1890s.

Trade also brought disease – smallpox, measles and typhoid – occasioning new epidemics with high mortality rates. And then in the 1890s rinderpest, a disease of cloven-hoofed animals, began to destroy herds of cattle on the Fipa Plateau as well as wild buffalo on the Rukwa Plain, contributing to food shortfalls only exacerbated by the irregular patterns of rainfall at the time. All this took its toll on the human population which suffered most on the Fipa Plateau and the forested interiors. The latter area was probably also scarred by the continuous raiding which forced farmers out of their homes and into the more secure fortressed villages.[68]

---

65. Waters (2009), p.67.

66. A palisaded fort was excavated in the village of Kibaoni, originally known as Kakuni. Foutch et al. (2009), p.258.

67. Tambila (1981), p.80-81.

68. Waters (2009), p.60.

Waters refers to these events of the late 1800s in Rukwa as occurring amidst an "ecology of fear".[69] He attributes three principal causes for this fear: frequent attacks on villages; trade in products such as guns, slaves and ivory; and the destruction of human populations through violence, disease and famine. As we mentioned above these conditions led to the reorganization of peoples and trade networks as subsistence societies grappled with the uncertainty and violence created by intruders from southern Africa and the Indian Ocean coast. One of the ecological effects of these developments was the desertion of the more remote countryside: as the elephant population diminished, farmers sought to stave off attacks from *ruga-ruga* by moving closer to the defended villages. The countryside became deserted. The space that this created may have contributed indirectly to the eventual establishment of parks and conservation land such as Katavi National Park.

Historians debate the effects of all these external forces on the region during the "Small Wars". Most agree that rural Africans were "being drawn into the world economy in accordance with someone else's economic goals, be they Arab, Asian or European."[70] Yet, while the needs of industrial nations in Europe were gradually dominating the developmental landscape, other historians stress that it would be wrong to view the western Tanzanian reaction as entirely passive in the face of outside influence. Far from being totally subordinate to the disturbances, new trading opportunities were seized upon by ambitious leaders keen to maximize development opportunities and stamp their personal authority over large areas. It was amongst such a hotbed of ambition and aggression that leaders emerged from the "Small Wars", battling to achieve hegemony both within and between tribal groups. Chiefs commanded allegiance from whomever they could, whether African, Arab or European, as they strove to attain political dominance. The vacuum of any dominant leader or status group at this time only served to compound the violence.[71]

The extent of economic development of the region during this period is also debatable. Many historians believe that the arrival of Arabs, Europeans and Indians, and the resulting dominance of cheaper, foreign goods, kept the region underdeveloped. Not only was local trade pushed out but the slave and ivory depredations of the Arabs stimulated tribal factionalism and violence as chiefs fought amongst one another to monopolize this trade. This school of historiography is contested by the ecological historian Dr. Helge Kjekshus who paints a more optimistic picture of a region not in economic free-fall or

---

69. Waters (2009), p.57-58. It is worth noting that these factional and geographical changes occurred in other regions of Tanzania as well as Rukwa.

70. Waters (2009), p.87.

71. Waters (2009), p.70-71.

ripped apart by internecine strife, but instead "full of indigenous economic vitality".[72] Kjekshus' argument is that imperialistic claims of a region torn apart by infighting, slavery, famine and disease were exploited by the Europeans to ideologically justify their intrusions and dominance. The European could claim that they were bringing peace and security to a hugely insecure region, allowing for both development and population growth.[73] The idea that this "violent" era may have been exaggerated by incoming supporters through the use of political cunning to whip up support may be true. However, given what we know of the time, Kjekshus' portrayal of a productive region that was not subjugated to the will of foreigners is possibly too optimistic to be taken at face value. Perhaps the truth lies somewhere between these two schools of thought: that alongside the political connivances of the "Small Wars", the region did develop economically to a certain extent although this was not ubiquitous and is likely to have been directed "by the needs of industrial production in far off lands."[74]

There is certainly no doubt that between the Ngoni's arrival from the 1840s until the 1880s, Rukwa was in a state of rapid change. Yet, it is worth remembering that the majority of people at this time were actually subsistence farmers growing crops both for themselves and their chiefs. Far from instigating violence, they simply "[produced the food which] underpinned the marauding chiefs, their armies and their courts."[75] These subsistence farmers were effectively forced to cede control of their production to chiefs who – in return for protecting the land – enforced levies and demanded foodstuffs. A stratified social system in Rukwa (and elsewhere) became entrenched by the need to protect crops, land and livestock as the outside world of global trade intruded.[76] Civilians paid a heavy price for this protection: not only did they sacrifice increasingly large parts of their material wealth to chiefs, but they were also forced to surrender their individual freedom and control of the production of their labour. This once again demonstrates the dominance of the ruling classes in 19th century Rukwa and their desire to maintain what was effectively a feudal society.

72. Kjekshus, H. Ecology Control and Economic Development in East African History: The case of Tanganyika, 1850-1950. Berkeley: University of California Press (1977).

73. Tambila (1981), p.21.

74. Tambila (1981), p.87-88.

75. Waters (2009), p.59.

76. Waters (2009), p.77.

CHAPTER THREE

MISSIONARIES, COLONIALS, AND CHIEFS

3.1 The Arrival of the German Military and French White Father Missionaries in Rukwa

By the 1890s, the "Small Wars" were drawing to a close, due in part to the declining ivory trade caused by the loss of elephants and the losses in human population resulting from famine and violence. The most important factor however was probably the arrival of the German colonialists and their alliance with the Catholic Order of Africa, a group of mostly French missionary priests, commonly known as the "White Fathers" due to the colour of their cassocks.[77]

The primary aim of the White Fathers was to establish mission stations to spread the Christian gospel. Cardinal Lavigerie founded the Society of Missionaries of Africa in 1878 after gaining permission from the Pope to work in the interior of Africa. Tambila believes that Lavigerie showed definite imperialist ambition in wanting to see the French colonize large areas south of the Sahara, and building a 'Christian kingdom.'[78] The priests first settled at Ujiji by Lake Tanganyika in 1879 but faced a hostile environment there. This was partly due to competition from the protestant London Missionary Society (although influence of this group proved to be limited and by 1893 they had left the area), but also due to entrenched Islam and Arab trading interests in the area. In 1885, the White Fathers established mission stations at Karema and Mpala, and in so doing ignited a slow but steady increase in Catholic missionary influence into Rukwa. They had purchased these stations from King Leopold's IAA, after its dissolution following the Conference of Berlin in 1885 and the resulting partition of Africa.

At the same time, the Germans were conquering East Africa, moving from the coastal belt in 1888, across the main caravan routes from 1890-1894, and then gradually extending westwards into Rukwa. This was a long drawn-out pattern of conquest and resistance, insofar as German incursions were "bitterly opposed by the invaded societies and could be forced through only over masses of dead resisters."[79] The Germans believed in using raw force to suppress any opposition they came into contact with. They based their approach on "social Darwinism", believing that they – as the superior force – were justified in dominating the inferior races in the interest of advancing civilization.[80]

---

77. They wore a white Berber Arab tract at a time when most priests wore black "soutaines."

78. Tambila (1981), p.91-92.

79. Tambila (1981), p.115.

80. Tambila (1981), p.115.

The Germans were bitterly resented but their advance could not be stopped. On 1st July 1890, Britain and Germany signed an Agreement to split the territories that were later to become known as Tanganyika and Northern Rhodesia into two.[81] After this treaty, in 1982, the Germans began a three point advance on the Rukwa area, from the south, the east and the north.[82]

From Lake Nyasa to the south, Major Hermann von Wissmann advanced toward the newly defined western boundaries of the German colony. Von Wissmann's ambition was to establish superiority over the peoples of the region, something which proved relatively easy with some of the petty chiefs yielding to him almost immediately. Von Wissmann also put down an uprising by the powerful chief Sunda, who lived to the south east of Lake Rukwa, with the assistance of mercenaries retained by chief Sunda's enemies. However, more typically, von Wissmann found himself in a bloody contest, fighting the chiefs and their *ruga-ruga* for each little piece of territory. He soon realized that he could not continue to sustain victories with his ever-depleting forces who were dying of hunger, injuries and disease. Luckily for the Germans, there were reinforcements in the area.

In the same year another expedition led by the German Captain Tom von Prince arrived from the east, moving through Ugongwe into the Rukwa Valley. However, both von Prince and von Wissmann together did not have the manpower to continue onto the Ufipa Plateau (even though von Prince did have some success in engaging and defeating the Fipa chief Kimalaunga and his followers who were forced to flee to the east of Lake Rukwa). Finally from the north came the German Captain Sigl and Lieutenant Bothmer. They had moved from Tabora to Ujiji and thence down the east coast of Lake Tanganyika, to Karema, which was to become the first military station.

Although the first German flags to be hoisted in this year had been subsequently trampled in the mud by the chiefs, the Germans formally declared the area to be under the auspices of the German empire on the 2nd September 1893. Subsequently, flags were ostensibly respected by the local chiefs, most probably in their bid to simply keep the Germans at bay. Kasanga which had been the original site of an ornithological research station established in 1888, was ultimately to become the principal town of the Germans in the west of their territory. It was renamed Bismarkburg in 1899 to reflect its military character.

There is no doubt that brutality played a large part in the German strategy of enforcing their will upon African society. Since their hold on the colony was relatively weak, they resorted to using violently repressive tactics to control the

---

81. Willis (1966), p.14.

82. Tambila (1981), p.121-127

population. Waters makes the point that German "ubiquity also freed the people of the incessant warfare between the chiefly castes,"[83] therefore putting a decisive end to the "Small Wars". In other words, the chiefs were so busy defending themselves against the Germans that they stopped fighting so much with each other.

Interestingly the Germans were helped enormously in their conquest by the assistance of the White Fathers, whom we introduced at the beginning of the chapter. For example, von Wissmann viewed the White Fathers as natural allies, delegating to the missionaries the task of drawing the more powerful chiefs into submission. He provided the White Fathers with guns and gunpowder (including a machine gun) as well as the promise of free passage for all missionaries on the German ship across Lake Nyasa.[84] The priests were mutually agreeable to this informal alliance, recognizing the opportunity that it presented in helping them to spread the Catholic gospel. In weakening the power of the chiefs, they saw the potential to indoctrinate the civilians with their own religious principles and way of life.

One clear example of the missionaries desire to work with the Germans is evident from the arrival, that we recounted earlier, of the German Captain Sigl and Lieutenant Bothmer in 1893. Their arrival at Karema was greeted with warmth by the White Fathers, who wrote,

"These German gentlemen are fired by good sentiment to us and, on our part, we are doing all we can to make them agreeable to us. Their presence cannot do anything else except rehabilitate our prestige in the eyes of the indigenous people. I am going to inform all the neighbouring chiefs to come the day after tomorrow to greet the representatives of the German empire and to submit their authority."[85]

The White Fathers also made a point of going publicly to church with the German military, symbolically unifying both sources of power.

The first White Fathers' mission station at Karema was, at once, a church, an important location for encouraging conversion to Catholicism, and a secure environment for visiting Europeans. Additionally, it became a refuge for escaped and redeemed slaves, along with refugees from the "Small Wars" and famine victims. These latter elements became part of the military army that the priests built up to protect themselves from disturbance and plundering raids, as well as to extend their Christian realm. These so-called "soldier catechists" (those who enforce the Christian message through violence) could use the large quantities of guns and gunpowder which the IAA had left behind, as well as those donated by German commanders. Soldier catechists assisted the White Fathers in suppressing those resistant chiefs who could not be converted through simple persuasion.

---

83. Waters (2009), p.72.

84. Tambila (1981), p.123-124.

85. Tambila (1981), p.127. This was taken from a White Father diary entry at Karema on 30.08.1893.

The chiefs' initial efforts focused on curtailing the movement and power of the White Fathers, and for a while, this worked. They found plenty of grounds for opposition. First, the chiefs perceived the Christian religion as one that was based on slaves since ex-slaves were used to help found the first missions. Second, they saw the missionaries as yet another group of outside traders; indeed, the missionaries organized regular caravan trips to the coast to collect European goods whilst also running shops at their stations which sold cheap cotton cloth – in fact by 1899, 800-1,000 loads of cloth were reaching the Karema mission annually. Third, the close cooperation between the priests and the German colonialists was regarded by some chiefs with considerable suspicion since they feared – quite rightly as it turned out – that they would effectively become pawns in the new power structure. Finally, some foresaw – again quite correctly – the threat of Christian ideology on their existing culture and beliefs, and particularly on the power of the chiefs themselves.[86]

We can see now that the chiefs were in many ways very perceptive about the potential consequences of the White Fathers and their new breed of religion for existing polities and societies. They worked successfully to stop the missionaries from building a church on the Ufipa Plateau until 1897, and also drove them out of Kirando several times. However, they could not ultimately prevent missionary advance in the long-term; the priests gradually expanded their territory and became increasingly involved in the administration of civil affairs. Between 1893 and 1912, several new missionary stations were opened, including one in Upimbwe, which will be discussed in more detail below.

3.2 Shifting Alliances Among Chiefs, Priests and German Colonials

The events in Upimbwe at the end of the 19th and beginning of the 20th century are useful for illustrating the growing influence of the newly arrived colonialists, particularly in how they dealt with chiefly quarrels. The conflict between chief Kalulu and chief Ngomayalufu demonstrates the problems they faced in subjugating the chiefs, despite their greater power. Recall that in Upimbwe, Kasogera's death in 1880 resulted in a succession crisis since he had eliminated all potential heirs. At this juncture, the chief's council decided to take power away from Kasogera, deeming that he came from a junior branch of the chiefly line, and had no legitimate right to the holding power. Instead, power was awarded to what they judged as the senior chiefly line, giving the position to the young Kalulu in the 1890s who at the time was living with his mother in Ugongwe.

Meanwhile, Kasogera's dispossessed line was smarting with anger at having had the chieftainship taken away from them. Accordingly, they took action by electing as chief Nsumba Mwananyima, who was a grandson of Kasogera and who inherited the name of Ngomayalufu. Acute tension gripped the Pimbwe chiefdom as the

---

86. Tambila (1981), p.98-99.

junior and senior branches of the chiefly lineage struggled for power. Since issues of succession were viewed as regional affairs, adjudication fell to the Tuutsi chief, Mwene Kapele of Nkansi; he was regarded as head of chiefs in the area which gives us some indication of the power that the more prosperous Fipa held over the Pimbwe at this time. This chief in turn was obliged to pass the case on to the new military station that the Germans had recently established at Bismarkburg on Lake Tanganyika.

The Germans initially awarded the chiefship to the young Kalulu since he represented the senior branch descending from Mfundo's line. However, they then changed track, ordering the chief of Nkansi to split the Pimbwe country between the two claimants, Kalulu and Ngomayalufu, probably around 1900. Kalulu was given the area comprising Mamba and the hot spring (at Pimbwe village) in the south, whilst Ngomayalufu was allocated the northern part which included Usevya. The boundary was at Mbede village. Ngomayalufu however objected to this decision, and consequently had his claim temporarily discarded; he was sentenced to nine months imprisonment in Kasanga.

Meanwhile Kalulu's violent nature and use of *ruga-ruga* was earning him an infamous reputation with the colonialists. Ngomayalufu took a chance to gain back German favour, and in the late 1890s answered the Germans' request to provide Pimbwe soldiers to assist with their retaliatory attack on the Bende to the north. Kalulu, on the other hand, provided no help. As a sign of their gratitude, in around 1900 the Germans gave Ngomayalufu ten villages lying between the Kavuu and Msadya rivers, slightly to the east of Kalulu's domain. Ngomayalufu continued to live at Usevya and, despite being told by the Germans that he was a subordinate to Kalulu, expanded his realm southwards right up to the border in Mbede.

Kalulu became increasingly nervous of the growing power to his north. He took the advice of a witch doctor (*mlodi*) who said that he must never shave his head without rubbing it first with a human heart (this was seen as a way to preserve power). Acting on this advice, the chief ordered two of his *ruga-ruga* to kill a man named Wamikamba and cut out his heart. This information reached the Boma (German government) at Kasanga, who responded by arresting Kalulu and sentencing him to fifty lashes and a long term of imprisonment. He only returned to Upimbwe many years later, where we will meet him again in his dealings with the White Fathers.

From the story of Ngomayalufu and Kalulu we see how the Germans used the rivalry that existed at this time between senior and junior branches of the Pimbwe royal family to divide the African people they were seeking to subjugate. However, the Germans were not alone in being manipulative. The Pimbwe chiefs similarly used the Germans to further their own interests,[87] as in Ngomayalufu's siding with the Germans against the neighbouring Bende in a bid to acquire more territory for himself.

---

87. Willis (1966), p.54.

More significant however were the longerterm consequences of this internecine struggle between the two Pimbwe chiefs. In their assertive division of the Pimbwe chiefdom between Kalulu and Ngomayalufu the Germans had taken a momentous step in weakening the Pimbwe realm, a step that led ultimately to the decline in the political power of Pimbwe chiefs.[88]

The Pimbwe however had not only to deal with the Germans but also the White Fathers. Various writings by missionary priests indicate that these priests moved into Upimbwe on 8th June 1904 under the guidance of Bishop Adolphe Lechaptois. They settled first at Usevya, near to the Msadya River, under Padre Gerard Wesnburg Ngalameka who was German, and his assistant Padre Kapela.[89] When the area was badly affected by flooding, all missionary buildings including the church were destroyed and the priests had to search for a new area to live. Under Ngalameka's guidance, they moved in 1906/07 to the hot spring area of Maji Moto which was, once more, under the jurisdiction of the chief Kalulu who had returned from prison and invited them to build in his village.

Picture 5. Monument to the first Catholic church built in Rukwa Valley in 1904 in Usevya.
Photo Monique Borgerhoff Mulder (2010).

88. Tambila (1981), p.72-73.

89. Oral interviews with Padre Mwiga and Daniel Kasike (2011). Padre Kapela (most likely Kappeler) was the assistant priest to Ngalameka. Although he was only an assistant, 'Kapela' in ki-Pimbwe means a person who is imbued with extremely important ritual power and so everybody thought that he was the supreme religious figure in the mission!

We believe Kalulu invited the missionaries because he feared attack from his archrival from Ufipa, the infamous ivory hunter chief Kimalaunga. The extra protection afforded to his territory by the missionaries and their guns was attractive. Lechaptois and his followers happily settled in the area and built their church within the palisades of Pimbwe village because it was close to a water source. Kalulu gave them a free reign to conduct their activities with minimal interference.

However, the affable relationship between the White Fathers and Kalulu soon soured when the priests destroyed a sacred stone (called *Mwakanakusima* or *Mpasa*), cut down a group of trees around the royal graves, and restricted the villagers from using the hot spring. A priest's donkey also ate Kalulu's crops. Each of these events seriously angered the chief. In response, he ordered the priests to be arrested and whipped for not showing reverence to a chief. He also threatened to make the hot spring dry up. The missionaries passed news of Kalulu's aggressiveness to the German colonial government who did not take his offence lightly and, in a sign of their authority, ordered him to move to a village four hours away. Meanwhile Kalulu resorted again to a witch doctor, this time named Mwana Kalembe, requesting certain rites to be performed that would cause trouble for the priests. The following year, 1910, there was an earthquake and the hot spring at Maji Moto dried up.[90] Kalulu read this as a sign that the spirits had answered his request. The priests were disturbed by the supposed 'spell' that had caused this turn of events and were forced to migrate to a village a few miles to the south, as recounted by Père Maurice who was stationed in Mpimbwe at the time.[91] The new village where the missionaries built their final church was named after the famous elder, Wamamba, who lived in the area.[92] The priests were happy to move to this beautiful spot under the escarpment, surrounded by trees and next to a spring with fresh water. Furthermore, they were welcomed by Wamamba, and in 1911 they constructed a church close to the site of the current one in Mamba village. The church is still very prominent today.

One school of thought relates that the missionaries had a difficult time in Mamba because the Pimbwe people regarded the whites as devils;[93] however, there is little to substantiate this claim. Nevertheless, back in Maji Moto village, the earthquake was seen as a sure sign that Pimbwe spirits were angered by the disrespect which the priests had shown to traditional areas of worship. The event particularly empowered chief Kalulu and, rather remarkably, in 1912 there was another earthquake which re-opened the spring, providing clear evidence for the

---

90. It is said locally that one missionary died from this earthquake, but there is no evidence of this in the written literature.

91. Père Maurice (1935), p.241-242.

92. Missionaries failed to pronounce *Wamamba* correctly and shortened it to Mamba, its present day name.

93. Tambila (1981), p. 103, citing a report for Utinta and Mpimbwe in 1908.

Pimbwe people of supernatural intervention on behalf of Kalulu. Kalulu re-asserted control of the villages to the east which had been awarded to Ngomayalufu (as discussed above). However although Kalulu did finally retain his power, the story of the White Fathers in Maji Moto demonstrates how the chiefs had to deal, albeit rather differently, with both German administrators and French missionaries as their positions became more fragile.

Picture 6. The rebuilt Catholic church in Mamba. Photo Monique Borgerhoff Mulder (2008).

As these events in Upimbwe have shown, this was a complicated time of shifting alliances and loyalties between the different parties, and in many parts of Tanzania the chiefs were holding out. For example, the early 1890s saw the Germans battling to bring the rebellious Hehe and Nyamwezi under control, and they had great difficulty in crushing a revolt by coastal Arabs in 1899. The year before this, the Germans had settled in Kasanga district but they did not appoint as executive officers *akidas*, the term for oppressive administrators assigned to groups of villages, as they had in most of the rest of German East Africa. The chiefs therefore continued to enjoy a relatively free reign in using *ruga-ruga* to subjugate their people and extract wealth and labour from them. In summary, what the Germans (together with the missionaries) achieved in this early period was relatively rapid control of intertribal warfare. They were less successful in stemming the intra-tribal depredations of some chiefs against their own peoples through the use of *ruga-ruga* and guns.[94]

---

94. Willis (1966), p.15. The *akida* system had originally been used by the Sultan of Zanzibar to rule his coastal subjects in east Africa. The Germans took it over and extended it inland.

3.3 Subjugation of the Chiefs

The final years of the 19th century saw a reluctant submission to German sovereignty with all the Westphalian political concepts that were imported from Europe without much reference to pre-existing local arrangements of rights and responsibilities. This was shown through the provision of soldiers when requested, and the payment of in-kind taxes to the German military government. This latter payment of tribute is interesting since it shows that the relationship between the subsistence farmer and the incoming German power was the same subservient one as that which had existed during the Small Wars under the powerful, manipulative chiefs.[95] However, taxation in particular caused much resistance, especially because Germans were unhappy about accepting in-kind payment of taxes, as we will discuss later. The chiefs of the Fipa Plateau and the Pimbwe also provided labour to build roads, took serious judicial disputes to German arbitration courts, and submitted to wearing German uniforms (particularly degrading as it was a daily reminder of both who was master of the area and of the increasing dependence on foreign goods). Those who protested were faced with whipping, fines, imprisonment and even execution, room for objection was almost non-existent.[96] In this section we trace the various developments, led by the colonial intruders or by the church, or both, which gradually undercut traditional authority.

One important theme was German brutality, as exemplified in the treatment given to the Fipa chief Kimalaunga who had been the cause of violent skirmishes during the "Small Wars", terrorizing the Fipa Plateau.[97] Kimalaunga was imprisoned by the Germans, and, in what his captors described as an escape attempt, was shot dead in 1899. He then had his head cut off and the Wafipa were ordered to bury the body. Kimalaunga had been known for his super-natural powers and, fearing that the body would transform into a lion and attack them, the Wafipa refused to get involved. As a result, prisoners were made to dig a grave and bury the corpse. The Germans clearly favoured publicly exploiting their defeat of this infamous ivory baron, using brutality to demonstrate their power and to defy anyone to oppose them.

Another important component in undercutting chiefly power was the commitment of the church to eliminate customs they viewed as abominable. As we saw earlier, the White Fathers recruited "soldier catechists", and used this corps in pursuit of their goal to abolish the custom of polygamy, to condemn chiefly fetishes and, perhaps most importantly, to stop the "trial by poison" ordeal which

---

95. Waters (2009), p.71.

96. Waters (2009), p.71.

97. He was said to have established alliances with groups of Nyamwezi, defeated 6,000 soldiers in Nkansi, his area of jurisdiction, and raided Lyangalile for cattle on a regular basis.

was an important prerogative of the chiefs.[98] At the mission station at Karema these redeemed slaves, orphans and others were also put to strenuous building and agricultural work. Their only payment was the promise of baptism, something the chiefs viewed as an additional direct threat to their power. The White Fathers were also committed to ending slavery and the slave trade, seeing this as pivotal to their attempt to bring the light of the gospel into what Livingstone had described as "darkest Africa."[99] They therefore encouraged commerce in goods other than slaves, something which could only be done if European nations became more directly economically and politically involved in the region. However, in this goal they were less effective. The slave trade was barely bruised by hostile outside influence, even after the Agreement to split Tanzania in 1890.[100] The Germans did make proclamations and pass laws trying to stop the practice, but in reality little changed on the ground; in fact slavery remained legal in mainland Tanzania until the British abolished it in 1923.[101] In this respect then, the church had little impact on the chiefs who benefited from slave trading.

Perhaps the most important impact of the missionaries on people in Mpimbwe and elsewhere in German East Africa was their establishment and control of educational institutions. Their influence was particularly effective at primary school level where orphans and other children were made to go to school and learn about the Christian religion. The priests insisted on education, and employed their "soldier catechists" to enforce missionary will. In Karema they also had a strong programme for educating girls, which was a focus right from the outset, and had strong effects on the functioning of Fipa families.[102] The missionaries also said that people should attend church, stop giving tributes and sacred offerings to the chief, and should worship God. For example, in Mamba, the White Fathers built a school which focused on religious training as well as reading and writing, and also established a vocational school for carpentry and masonry. This gradually led to a caucus of individuals starting to believe more in the power of the church rather than the chief.

This introduction of new western European cultural values into the region clearly threatened to destroy traditional Pimbwe culture, and to weaken the power of the chiefs who represented the pinnacle of this culture. Chiefs had always been rulers of their subjects, protectors against foreign attacks and brokers in their

---

98. Trial by poison was where the chiefs gave a special medicine to someone whose loyalty they questioned. This was viewed as an oath or a pledge and was used as a judgment for people who did wrong in society: it was believed that if the person behaved badly and had not complied with the chief's wishes they would die, but they would survive if innocent.

99. Tambila, (1981), p.91.

100. Willis (1966), p.xv, see also Deutsch, Jan-Georg. Emancipation without Abolition in German East Africa, c.1884-191. Oxford: James Currey (2006).

101. Villagers in Kibaoni village reported that the last redeemed slave in their village had died in about 1997.

102. Smythe, K.R. Fipa Families. New Hampshire: Heinemann (2006), p.76.

people's quarrels; now things were changing. Much to the chiefs' frustration, they could do little to put a stop to the "cultural and ideological reorientation of the societies" that the missionaries were encouraging.[103]

It is difficult to tell whether the Pimbwe disliked the missionaries or the Germans more. Clearly the Pimbwe were appalled by the disrespectful behaviour of the White Fathers in Maji Moto, when for example sacred graves were destroyed. They also strongly resented proselytization for its negative effects on tribal beliefs and customs, and were irritated by priests who made them spend so much time carrying out church duties. But dislike for the German colonialists, and their brutal behaviour, seems to have been more acute. Indeed, Roland Oliver warns of the dangers of very anti-imperialist writings that make no attempt to differentiate between the relatively benign roles of missionaries and the harsh German soldiers.[104] It is likely, however, that initially friendly relations between Pimbwe and missionaries cooled when the latter tried to interfere with the Pimbwe way of life. Furthermore many local chiefs viewed the priests as working "in league" with the Germans. As Tambila concludes, the missionaries were viewed as representatives of the Germans, and that they had to be kept out at all cost.[105]

The key point for our present focus on the subjugation of the chiefs, however, is that the combined pressure of both missionaries and the German military tested the ordinary people's traditional loyalties. The situation was aggravated by the beleaguered chiefs' increased use of trial by poison as they tried to apply moral pressure to re-assert authority over their subjects. Père Maurice recounts increasingly whimsical use of power by chiefs during his first visit to Mpimbwe in 1906. He notes chiefly use of witchcraft to terrorize subjects, to demand shares of all meat hunted in the country, all beer brewed from its grain, and all fish caught in its rivers. Witchcraft was also used to make unreasonable demands for women (even married women), with the priest making reference to a harem of twenty wives. Clearly the chiefs were making a threatening use of authority based on fear.[106]

Intriguingly these actions had the opposite of the desired effect. Not only did they serve to distance the fearful subjects from their chief, but also the simultaneous extension and reduction of chiefly powers made commoners question chiefly judgment. Gradually some people started to rely on protection from the Germans to oppose chiefly privileges, for example, in not providing the tusk from every elephant killed to the chief of that area as tradition dictated that they should. Accordingly, whilst some subjects did flee from particularly harsh colonial rulers, others actually joined hands with their oppressors – the chiefs – to oppose the Germans. It is likely that they did so in part because they saw chiefs

---

103. Tambila, (1981), p.90, 129.

104. Oliver, R. The Missionary Factor in East Africa (1966), p.95.

105. Tambila (1981), p.127-128.

106. Père Maurice (1935), p.230-232.

as semi-deities,[107] in part because chiefs always had, and were well-placed to, make defensive forays against invaders, and in part because colonialist demands were very often much harsher than those made by the chiefs. Moreover there was sometimes scope for the chief's subjects to influence their leader, whereas such flexibility did not exist under the oppressive German rule.[108]

At the same time, colonial administrative power was markedly stepped up, with the Germans establishing a military post at Ujiji in 1895. In August 1896, Commander von Ramsay, stationed at Ujiji, ordered new regulations including regular school attendance with religious instruction and the total ban of trial by poison – those caught still practicing the custom would be arrested and hanged. The Germans also established their own courts to hear cases, directly bypassing the chiefs. The colonialists also stipulated that each chief should plant one hundred trees each year in his area (such as banana trees, mango trees, or oil palms), and that the chiefs should come and visit the missionaries in Karema from time to time, making the journey as a mark of their subservience to the white people. At the same time, the Ordinance of 1896 prevented chiefs from collecting taxes or tribute from their subjects, and also from imposing death sentences, perhaps their most powerful weapon against their subjects.[109] As a result of the unpopularity of these orders, the Germans tried to restrict the ownership of firearms, fearful of the uprisings that might occur if their supply was left unchecked. However, their efforts were limited because local craftsmen had already started to manufacture their own guns and produce their own gunpowder from pyrite found in the hillsides. Sometimes, young men were required to provide guns as an essential part of the bride wealth. Many potential bridegrooms found it difficult to accumulate this wealth, the effect of which was a tighter control by elders over boys and girls.

In 1894, the colonialists began the process of taxation in efforts to make the colony economically viable, and to make the people produce oil products for export to Germany.[110] Their intention was also to supply labour for colonial infrastructure (such as telegraph lines, mission stations, and plantations), and to educate Africans as citizens for whom tax was a part of everyday life. Between 1894 and 1897, efforts to introduce tax were thwarted due to very dry weather and an invasion of locusts which destroyed most people's harvest. An Ordinance was signed on 1st November 1898 which imposed a "House and Hut tax"[111] across the whole country, but

---

107. Père Maurice (1935), p.228.

108. Père Maurice (1935), p.141.

109. It is unlikely that these orders were actually read out, but chiefs quickly grasped the meaning of them and the detrimental effect that they would have on the power they wielded over their people.

110. These included groundnuts (peanuts), coconuts and sesame seeds.

111. Black Africans were to pay the 'hut' tax, whilst the 'house' tax would be paid by other races.

even then it was not officially collected in Rukwa until 1900. This is perhaps best explained by Governor Liebert, who was in charge at the time and observed that,

> *"[t]he English administration ... and also the Portuguese administration, our neighbouring colonies, have already had to fight extensive wars because of their roughness in the introduction of the head tax. It will be an important part of the instructions to give directions in this respect and to recommend the highest degree of care."[112]*

The Germans were therefore particularly careful not to provoke rebellion close to the neighbouring European colonies of the Belgian Congo and British-governed Northern Rhodesia, or in areas under military rule, because they feared losing territory in the resulting civil disobedience.

Aside from John Iliffe's claim that tax proved easy to collect,[113] there is general agreement that resistance was widespread and heartfelt. People strenuously objected to paying taxes on the grounds that this would change the whole socio-economic fabric of their way of life. One clear sign of this resistance is that so little tax was actually collected, with amounts decreasing rather than increasing in the early years of the 20th century. People had without doubt learned very quickly how to avoid paying. Although von Liebert (the Governor of German East Africa at the turn of the century) played down opposition to this German policy in letters he sent to Berlin, there seems little doubt that the military had to resort to much brutality to stifle disobedience and impose colonial taxation. Indeed, people risked facing mistreatment, the burning of their house, or death if they refused to pay their taxes in a policy focused intently on introducing regular money into the economy.[114]

It is interesting that – in the face of potential opposition and without the manpower required for tax collection - the Germans cunningly tried to exploit their missionary ties in asking them to collect the tax for them. But although recognizing the value of this tax, the White Fathers also acknowledged its unpopularity. Viewing the German request as a strange demand they refused to assist the Germans, and in doing so maintained some heretofore unobserved independence and demonstrated their refusal to bend to every colonial wish. There was clearly a limit to their imperial cooperation. It was only in 1899 after the military station at Bismarkburg had been properly set up that the Germans had the appropriate administrative system in place to carry out tax collection.

For example, in later years of the German administration, this included the use, or even exploitation, of deposed chiefs such as Kapere of Nkansi (who the Germans had deposed in 1905). Kapere was initially sent to small chiefdoms

---

112. Tambila (1981), p.151.

113. Iliffe (1979), p.133.

114. Tambila (1981), p.159-160.

such as Mpimbwe, Urawila and Rungwa to explain to people how to pay tax. He had both a secretary and a police escort to assist him in this task which gives some idea of the unpopularity of tax collection. Since the colonialists had limited manpower on the ground, the efforts of chiefs like Kapere were vital in helping to keep German rule legitimate. They were paid relatively large sums of money, showing the importance that the Germans attached to tax collection and the monetization of the economy.[115] Even the chiefs viewed their role with much importance, with Kapere admitting that he had "acquired a big head for getting so much money."[116] However, in becoming loyal vassals to the Germans, the chiefs could no longer claim to be a leader in the traditional sense of the word. They became very unpopular for submitting to a foreign power, which again contributed to chiefly decline. At the same time, Kapere's involvement shows that an alliance of sorts had been formed between chief and invading power instead of the hostile and distrusting relationship that invariably developed between the two. Ironically, whilst the Germans could not influence the priests where tax was concerned, they could influence some chiefs.

Once taxation did take effect, it proved yet another resource which the Germans could call upon to demonstrate their strength. Salt and gun taxes were introduced which caused much dislike,[117] and in 1905 the "house and hut tax" was replaced with a "head tax" upon all males. Whilst the 1905 Ordinance allowed payment, it was discouraged because the Germans did not want to receive grain that had been poorly stored. From 1907, the government ordered that taxes were to only be collected in cash rather than foodstuffs.[118] This presented the African peasant with great difficulties because very often their only means of payment was food crops. They had nowhere to store their grain to prevent it from rotting or becoming infested with pests, and the administration maintained no grain stores for the communities. It is possible that Governor von Liebert's order that workers should be paid their salaries and food in cash (rupee) from 1899 had some positive effect in providing workers with more ready cash, but we have no way of being certain about this.[119] It is also possible that the Germans initially accepted some food as payment in kind even if it was likely to rot. By the early years of the 20th century however, taxation in cash was recognized as an important tool for injecting money into the economy, and opponents were dealt with harshly. This is seen nowhere clearer than from

---

115. Tambila (1981), p.157.

116. Tambila (1981), p.157.

117. Guns were becoming an important part of the bride wealth when a young man got married. They were also significant for hunting and supplying proteins in areas with few cattle. The salt tax meant that salt collection interfered with the regional trade network and made it difficult for people to buy the required daily intake of salt.

118. Tambila (1981), p.151, 184.

119. We do know that African porters were usually paid in kind, either with the preferred item of cloth, or with beads or powder. It is likely that it would have taken their employers some time before they began to pay their porters with real money.

Governor von Götzen's response to a critic in 1906, "The suggestion that taxing the blacks should be given up is tantamount to abandoning the colony."[120]

Harassment of chiefs by the Germans continued into the 20th century and occurred in many parts of German East Africa. Chiefs frequently faced humiliation and imprisonment such as when they tried to assert their own power through stealing cattle from their subjects. The typical colonial policy of total confrontation was to prove problematic in that it involved defeating and disgracing the very people, the chiefs, whom the Germans would need as potential allies to help control the common people. Meanwhile, as old intra-tribal rivalries continued to flare up, chiefs mistakenly believed that they could play a rival group off against the Germans and win. The Germans exploited such chiefly naïvety, so that instead of organizing any meaningful resistance, the chiefs' energies were often wasted in court intrigue. At the same time, the wake of natural disasters in the 1890s such as the rinderpest epidemic and famines due to locust invasions and drought weakened the existing system further and made colonial conquest easier.[121]

The situation came to a head with the Maji Maji rebellion (1905 - 1907)[122] which was focused primarily in the southern part of German East Africa. Maji Maji represented African resistance to German policies, and was the greatest challenge to German colonial rule in Africa. The Tanzanian people particularly objected to the policy of forced labour to build roads, as well as the insistence that each village should grow cotton as a cash crop for export. The production of cotton was extremely unpopular since men were often away from their homes working, and it fell to women to take on the traditional male roles such as farming. The social fabric of society was changing, the result of which was that women had little time to do their other work. Consequently, over-stretched families struggled to get enough food and remain self-sufficient. This combination of factors, plus the drought in 1905, pushed people to the limit and led to open rebellion against the Germans in July of that year. The Germans were fearful of this uprising and sent many troops, even from Rukwa territory, down to the south and south east of German East Africa to fight the Maji Maji. Although the African rebels did have some successes during the uprising and destroyed a few smaller garrisons, the Germans ultimately prevailed because they requested reinforcements which arrived both from the German government and from New Guinea. Their fortifications and modern weapons were also superior to the poorly armed Africans who had to make do with spears and arrows, and did no always attack in a coordinated fashion.

Around the same time as the unrest that led to the Maji Maji rebellion, resistance to colonial rule stirred in Lyangalile at the centre of Ufipa. Their chief, Kundawantu,

---

120. Tambila (1981), p.149.

121. Tambila (1981), p.66.

122. Maji Maji which means "water" in ki-Swahili was named after the "war medicine" that the spirit medium, Kinjikitile Ngwale (or Bokero as he called himself) gave to his followers. He said that this "war medicine", which comprised of water mixed with castor oil and millet seeds would turn German bullets into water.

cooperated with the Germans for a few years before becoming particularly aggressive in trying to re-establish the traditional rights of chiefs. He also led widespread opposition to the head tax that, as discussed above, the colonialists tentatively tried to introduce on the people of Rukwa in 1898. Kundawantu's family were held hostage in response to his resistance but he put up a great fight and engaged in many skirmishes, only being arrested after he was tracked down by spies in 1906 and then publicly hanged. Whilst there is no direct evidence of a link between these protesters and the Maji Maji fighters, the news of Maji spread through Tabora all the way to Mwanza so the resisters would most probably have heard about it. The fighting in Lyangalile certainly seems to have been rooted in its own causes, but there it is likely that people in Ufipa were strengthened in their fight against the colonialists by news of the disquiet that was gradually bubbling up in the south-east. It is interesting that Roy Willis sees this hanging as marking the end of any independent states on the Fipa Plateau.[123]

Meanwhile in Ubende, which lies just to the north of Upimbwe, Major Ramsay's 1896 orders barely impacted upon the society. For this reason, August Fonck, the new German commander in Kasanga, interposed directly. In 1900 he ordered that small villages were to be merged with bigger ones, all children were to attend mission schools, and girls could not be married off before reaching marriageable age. Equally, all adults were to undergo catechism classes and were forbidden from leaving these classes without permission from the priest in charge of the mission station. This weakening of parental control and erosion of chiefly powers was defied by the alliance of two Bende chiefs, Katunka and Kabulola, who resorted to the trial by poison ordeal in which many people died. Katunka had built up his defences by recruiting Bende elephant hunters to help him and purchasing large amounts of gunpowder from rubber merchants, but the two chiefs could not cope with the German strength under Commander Fonck which included mercenaries from the Mpimbwe and Rungwa. Although not defeated completely, the Bende chiefs were forced to accept German superiority. This is yet one more example of how the Germans reigned in the powers of the chiefs.[124] Ultimately the undemocratic Europe of the 19th and early 20th century inspired German desire for total supremacy over any opposition, and encouraged their colonial administrators to use more violence than ever deployed to oppress the German state of the time.[125]

Exhausted by their own fighting and unable to compete with German firepower, the chiefs grudgingly submitted to German rule. Opposition had largely been broken by 1907, although the German colonialists continued to face pockets of resistance until 1913 whilst Rukwa was still under military administration. By the end of the first decade of the 20th century the power of the chiefs crumbled enormously, but we should remember that – in trying to defend their own powers

123. Willis (1981), p.211-214.

124. Tambila (1981), p. 137

125. Tambila (1981), p. 138

– they often did not help themselves. Whether it was through African disunity which frequently led to renewed defeat from the more organized German attacks, the human sacrifice made by chief Kalulu in an attempt to preserve his own authority, or the illegitimate use of trial by poison, the chiefs only weakened their own status further. In doing so, the chiefs unwittingly helped to cement German colonial conquest in western Tanzania, a conquest that had been facilitated, intentionally or not, by the works of the White Fathers.[126]

3.4 Rukwa Becomes a Labour Reserve

In 1903, Rukwa had been characterized as "the dead looking corner of the protectorate at the southern end of Lake Tanganyika."[127] Eight years later, in 1911, the change was remarkable; as one White Father missionary observed, people had acquired "a love for money." Their desire to earn rupees was a key catalyst for encouraging the emigration of workers to become road or railway builders, or work on the coastal plantations. There are a number of reasons which help us to understand why Rukwa became a labour reserve. Some are linked to the people's desire to earn more money, whilst others provide us with an indication of the hostile economic and social environment that they faced back home in Rukwa.

First, the traditional economies of iron and cloth were undercut by cheap imports. This meant that the pre-colonial production and exchange system could not function successfully in its original format. Second, the Germans banned the peoples of Rukwa from growing cash crops such as cotton, sisal, rice, oil palm and peanuts on their own private farms (or *shamba*, Kiswahili) as they were too successful at running them and crucially the Government wanted to stifle productivity in the region. All the local people could sell was honey and fish. The government also imposed a system of collective farming, where people worked for the public (often government) not personal benefit, and which the people resented bitterly; ultimately they refused to carry out such unproductive work.[128]

Third, the demands for greater taxation became a heavy burden. Between 1900 and 1905, the amount of tax collected was minimal. However, from 1906, it rose considerably, no doubt aided by colonial pressure since Germany had by now recognized the significant role it could play in monetising the economy.[129] By 1909/1910, taxes had reached around 20,000 rupees. The situation was compounded by the fact that from 1907, as noted above, Commander Fonck insisted that taxes were collected only in cash. Those who had no cash tried to sell

---

126. Waters (2009), p.74. It is of interest that the White Fathers were the most consistent foreign presence in a remote region where the outside political powers changed frequently. Between 1870 and 1970, political shifts moved from indigenous chiefs to German military officers, to British colonial officers and finally the independent Tanzanian government. The White Fathers presence did not disappear until the 1980s and, whilst few remain to this day, the church they established remains strong and significant.

127. Tambila (1981), p.152.

128. Tambila (1981), p.169.

129. Planters, farmers and even missionaries had also realised the importance of taxation by this time.

goats or other foodstuffs in return for cash, but this was problematic in itself since most households already owned these commodities and those who didn't lacked the money to purchase them anyway.[130] Fourth, the peasants were keen to rid themselves of the exactions and hardships imposed on them by petty chiefs as the latter strived, increasingly unsuccessfully, to maintain their position of dominance in an increasingly changing world. Finally, the cattle herds on the Ufipa Plateau had largely been destroyed owing to the rinderpest epidemic which had begun in the 1890s. The fact that very few cattle had survived only further weakened the farming economy.

For all these reasons out-migration for cash labour on the coast seemed a good solution. Furthermore, vigorous recruitment operations took place. The Germans welcomed these recruiters. They could work with the recruiters, whether these were planters, miners, or railway contractors, to exert yet more control over the livelihoods of the peasants. By 1911, recruiters, often of Greek, Arab or Indian origin, had come to Mpimbwe all the way from Korogwe in the Tanga region, promising twelve rupees a month which was a huge sum of money.[131] These recruiters were reportedly frequently harsh in their efforts to compel Africans to work.[132] Abuses extended to burning huts or capturing domestic animals, and one particularly notorious incident occurred when a Greek recruiter in Usevya sexually assaulted a woman in 1912. In Mpimbwe, recruiters were called "devils" and railway building was known as "the work of the devil"; to avoid being recruited for railway work men would hide or even cross the lake to Congo.

Wage labour nevertheless formed a fundamental link for the Rukwa Valley to the colonial economy drawing men into multiple types of employment. As well as the different cash crop plantations on the coast, there were hundreds of public work projects which required labour such as the building of roads, bridges and waterways, and mining enterprises, as well as the numerous domestic opportunities, working as cooks and house-boys for higher level employees. It is fair to say that the inhabitants of Rukwa became much more heavily involved in labour migration compared to those in other regions.[133] By 1911, about 10 out of 100 men were migrating from Mpimbwe to places such as Korogwe, Morogoro, Tabora and Muheza. The region had taken on all the characteristics of a labour reserve. Bishop Lechaptois and his missionaries were very concerned about the effect of emigration on their Christian aims for the region. They worried that the high level of depopulation would ruin Christian and

---

130. Tambila (1981), p.155.

131. Tambila (1981), p.184, 188.

132. These white recruiters also depended on Africans who resided in the target villages to act as the ultimate re-cruiters. The Africans were not traditional chiefs, but were picked from among the villagers or brought in from outside. Without them, the whites would not have been so successful because they did not know the terrain well.

133. Tambila (1981), p.188.

family life because only women remained in some villages. Ironically, insofar as the missionaries' on-going efforts in promoting monogamy and nuclear families had already loosened the extended family, men faced fewer constraints in leaving their wives and children, though the situation for the remaining women and children was probably even worse, without strong extended family help. Lechaptois urged the German administration to take a stance, but at the time of his writing in 1913, the District Officers were already indirectly facilitating emigration, both by taxing remaining inhabitants heavily and ignoring most reports of abuse by recruiters. Upon the arrival of World War I in 1914, labour migration had become a permanent part of the regional economy. Rukwa was now a significant labour supplier, particularly for the coastal plantations but also for railway construction projects.[134]

The migrant labour flow out of Rukwa had three hard-hitting effects. It led to a significant population decrease which was made worse by the fact that many men did not return home to their families,

"Tabora, Tanga, Dar es Salaam are veritable colonies of the Pimbwe. Furthermore, they do not get satisfied with one year of this unsettled life. Only too often do they pass five or six years without returning to their country."[135]

The absence of men led to a reduction in the birth rate, as well as a gradual increase in promiscuity and abortions; abortions were dangerous, often resulting in sterility (or death) for women, and promiscuity facilitates the spread of sexually transmitted diseases, which can also lower rates of fertility. For the men working on the labour plantations and railway construction sites, life was also not easy. Mortality rates were shockingly high: on the sisal plantations, for example, the average annual death rate was between 7 and 10% of the total employed annually, and often much higher due to the appalling health conditions.[136] This must in part explain why approximately 20% of those who emigrated from Mpimbwe before 1914 had not returned four years later.

The second effect was the ruination of family life brought about by the continued absence of 20-40 year old men. The custom that a woman should not remarry until the confirmed death of her husband led to a climate in which prostitution, unwanted pregnancies and abortion became regular occurrences. In Mpimbwe, women were forced into polygamy – often required to marry a wealthy older man after needing to borrow money from him in order to support themselves without their husbands' wages; in this form of transactional sex women become dependent clients on men who acted as patrons. However, even marrying an older man soon became difficult because the villages were almost devoid of any marriageable men at all:[137]

---

134. Tambila (1981), p.185,187.

135. Tambila (1981), p.196.

136. Tambila (1981), p.197-198.

137. Some of the elderly women in Mpimbwe remember hearing from their mothers how very few men resided in the villages during this period.

Thirdly, the region suffered considerable economic degeneration owing to the loss of its most economically active men. Not only did their absence reduce food production (thus obviating any possibility of food export from the region) but government officials wanted the region to continue as a labour reserve. With this in mind, they sought to keep the region underdeveloped, not only as we have seen by pushing taxes up and quietly assisting recruiters, but also by the prohibition on growing cash crops such as cotton which could have boosted its economic vitality. The result was that trade faltered, and there was no incentive for a farmer to increase his or her agricultural production. The German Governor von Rechenberg recognized that the difficulties faced by the Pimbwe arose largely from colonial plantation policy, but his proposed solution (to support both the interests of big capital and the peasant farmers) was not well accepted by the imperial capitalists in Berlin. Consequently, underdevelopment of the region persisted. Rukwa remained as a labour reserve, with the local people trapped in a vicious economic circle.

The labour reserve period had caused great problems for the people of Rukwa, but the outbreak of World War I only exacerbated the situation. Although not directly involved, Africans played a vital part as carriers and suppliers of food. Each white man fighting in the war needed ten carriers or African *askari* (soldiers, Kiswahili) to transport his arms, medical supplies and food, as well as two or three personal servants. For example, the German offensive, which took place between August 1914 and May 1916, involved about 3,500 Germans for the whole of German East Africa and required some 42,000 supporting Africans. By 1917, the British invaders employed 175,000 carriers, as did the Belgians who also invaded at around the same time. Although no one can be certain, it is likely that ninety per cent of these recruits came from German East Africa.[138] Whilst many were labourers who had been working on cash crop plantations, railways or other large businesses, demand for carriers and suppliers became so great that the army started to conscript non-labourers. The men in places like Rukwa were in even greater demand than ever.

---

138. Tambila (1981), p.207, who cites the last German Governor in German East Africa, Heinrich Schnee, as describing the African participation in the war as "enormous."

CHAPTER FOUR

BRITISH RULE

4.1 World War I and the Coming of the British

The coming of World War I brought Britain, Belgium, and South African forces to Rukwa. The Germans were under constant retreat from these armies. During this period, Rukwa became split between the British and the Belgians. By 1916, the British occupied the southern part of former Bismarkburg – the Lake Tanganyika coast up to Cape Mpimbwe (now known as Msalaba), the Ufipa Plateau and the Rukwa Valley. The northern part of Bismarkburg fell to Belgian occupation between 1916 and 1920, headquartered at Kigoma.

In this wartime period the Germans, Belgians, and British all moved through the Rukwa region at one point or another which made areas like Mpimbwe, Ufipa and the Rukwa Valley lose virtually all their remaining men. Serving as either combatants or carriers of supplies, these men suffered heavily from injuries, disease, hunger and exhaustion. The inhabitants remaining in Rukwa did little better. Armies lived off the land and conscripted local labour to supply them with food. Since all the men were either at war, or away working on plantations and railways, pressure fell on those left behind – the women and children – to provide the army with meat, grain and oils. It was this which made African participation in the war by both men and women all encompassing.

World War I had many terrible effects as well as depopulation. Because troops and carriers had to live off the land, war was by necessity conducted in populated areas. As troops passed through villages, they caused havoc, burning and plundering villages and destroying crops in the field. The army's justification for such destruction was that nothing of any value be left, should these areas fall into enemy hands. The burning of villages and the consequent destruction of grain storage and field crops contributed to severe and widespread famine. The local people came increasingly short of food, depending on the production of women alone.[139] The result of this was that health conditions deteriorated significantly, only exacerbated by the constant movements of men and animals across the countryside which facilitated the spread of disease. Indeed, Spanish influenza, dysentery, smallpox and pneumonia were all endemic by 1918 (and persisted until the 1930s).

To make matters worse taxation was still compulsory, and women even had to pay anything their absent husbands, fighting in the war, owed. The women struggled a lot with this burden although may have been helped a little by the fact

---

139. Tambila (1981), p.211.

that local manufacturing somewhat revived itself during the war. Imports were not possible during the conflict so certain crafts, such as the production of iron and "seketa" cloth started up again. [140] The colonial economy had not completely succeeded in destroying these traditional skills, allowing the inhabitants of the region to quickly resume some of their old local manufacturing work. [141] It is interesting to note that "seketa" production was not re-ignited because of policy decisions, but on account of the initiative of the people themselves. Soon, demand became so high that supply could not properly keep pace.

The conflict between Europeans in Africa during World War I had not just economic but political and even psychological consequences. The invading Europeans who sought to control the land through fighting each other only made the Africans despise them further. Chiefs tried to use this situation to reassert their sovereignty, with some demanding back land which had been taken over by the missionaries. Threats to missionaries were perceived as a direct way of challenging European conquest. Church and mission attendance plummeted. By 1916 and 1917, the White Fathers could no longer wield the same influence or power over traditional chiefs and their people as they had previously.

With the end of the war and the Treaty of Versailles (1919) the Germans lost their territories in East Africa, most of which were handed to Great Britain to be administered as a Mandate under the League of Nations, with the name of Tanganyika. [142] In 1920, the Belgians retreated entirely from western Tanganyika, handing over sovereignty to the British under the Milner-Orts Agreement. That same year, British administrators arrived in Rukwa to take up governance. As had the Germans almost thirty years earlier, the British struck up a close alliance with the French White Fathers. The British strategy was otherwise very different from that of the Germans. They were short of capital, depended heavily on cheap African labour, and made no effort to invest in Tanganyika as their predecessors had done in some parts of the realm with respect to railways and plantations. They also favoured a policy of "indirect rule" which allowed Rukwa to be ruled by Africans for the first time since its military occupation in 1898.

Tanganyika's second British Governor, Sir Donald Cameron, was a politically liberal individual. Considered to be the greatest name in the history of British rule in Tanganyika, [143] he arrived in 1925 and immediately stressed his belief in indirect rule which he called Local Native Administration,

---

140. Locals used cotton to make "seketa", a kind of shawl woven on primitive hand looms.

141. Tambila (1981), p.216-217.

142. Willis (1966), p.xv.

143. Hughes, A.J. East Africa: Kenya, Tanzania Uganda. London: Penguin Books (1969), p.45.

*"The intention [is] to administer Africans as far as possible through the
instrument of their own indigenous systems instead of directly through the
administrative officer ... It is our duty to do everything in our power to develop
the native on lines which will not westernize him and turn him into a bad
imitation of a European."*[144]

Under Native Ordinances implemented during the 1920s, it was the role
of each chief, headman (*jumbe*) or council of elders to maintain law and order
without the presence of uniformed soldiers and police. The local administrators
also took over responsibility for collecting taxes, implementing agricultural,
fisheries and forestry policy, as well as running primary and middle schools. In
short, the British maintained a policy of minimum direct interference.

Under Cameron and in an effort to stimulate trade, the British organized
their East African peoples as "tribes", ensuring that they picked chiefs who were
legitimate and submissive, and who could rule their "tribes."[145] In spite of this,
the powerful preexisting independent chiefs, who employed *ruga-ruga* and
still claimed the right to conduct trials, did their best to continue under British
colonialism. However, the Governor, the Provincial Commissioners and the
District Commissioners were always in ultimate control. The irony of "indirect
rule" was that, in the end, the chiefs became mere "symbols in the context of a
more powerful British colonial government:"[146] For example, in 1944 the Pimbwe
chief Nsokolo II, his court officers and *ruga-ruga* sacrificed a boy whose body was
then mixed with sheep or goat meat, turned into a stew and served to the villagers.
Sacrifice had long been a chiefly strategy to demonstrate power, and Nsokolo's
feast marked an attempt to reassert authority. However, his plan was thwarted
as villagers, now disenchanted with such activities, reported the incident to the
British. The District Commissioner arrested Nsokolo and his court; they were
jailed in Kasanga before eventually being sent to Tabora where they were tried
and hung.[147] This execution was greeted with approval by the villagers, and most
likely marked the last independent example of royal prerogative in Mpimbwe.

Aside from chiefs, it appears that whilst the Native Authorities handled small
criminal cases themselves, acts such as killings and the burning of property would
have been passed to colonial authorities. The Native Authorities sensed their
vulnerability, for they could have their powers reduced or be fired at will should
the British wish to do so. The British also worked hard to effectively abolish both
the practice and the institution of slavery which, as has been mentioned, they
successfully did in 1923.

---

144. Hughes, (1969), p.45-46.

145. Waters (2009), p.72.

146. Waters (2009) p.75.

147. Waters (2009), p.73-74.

Sir Donald Cameron's long-term aim was to encourage self-rule and eventual independence for Tanganyika. He believed that education would be the key to his success, and therefore set about reforming the education system. In spite of increasing the number of pupils in Government schools ten-fold, and the amount of money spent eight-fold between 1925 and 1931, there were still not enough schools or places to accommodate children. Cameron therefore sought help from the missionaries who only charged half the cost of Government schools to provide education. The missionaries nevertheless failed to provide vocational education in remote areas such as Rukwa, where it was so critical. There were a few masons, carpenters and blacksmiths but, as the 1925 Namanyere Annual Report makes clear,

"many of these are far from skilled and their appellation 'fundi' is often only self-given and at the best means that they have for a short while at some remote period assisted a master craftsman."[148]

Overall, Cameron's well-meaning policy was impeded by the economic depression at the end of the 1920s and by his focus on tribalism which perhaps hindered local communities in acquiring the western skills they needed to navigate colonial policies. His liberal policy, whilst well-meaning, was well ahead of its time, and he departed as Governor in 1931. His less competent successors were unable to maintain pressure on improving educational standards, evident from the fact that the total spent on education fell from £111,302 or 6.36% of total revenue in 1930/31 to £92,313 or 3.94% of revenue in 1937.[149] Indeed, the concern of the League of Nations can be seen when, in 1938, its Permanent Mandates Commission chastised the British delegate for the very poor expenditure on African education. Sadly, Cameron's efforts in this sphere had been in vain.

The conflict that has been touched upon earlier between Ngomayalufu and Kalulu re-emerged during British rule. When World War I had broken out, Kalulu went into hiding so that he did not have to sign up for military service, only returning once the Belgians had taken control of Maji Moto and the surrounding area in 1916. Ngomayalufu on the other hand was recruited first by German troops, then captured by the British at Kisaki, and finally interned at Morogoro.[150] Returning to Mpimbwe after the end of the war Ngomayalufu asked for permission to build a new village; this was granted, provided that he kept to his side of the chiefly boundary at Mbede. However, in 1921 he cultivated and built huts across the boundary which greatly angered Kalulu who responded by complaining to

---

148. Ufipa District Annual Report from Namanyere Administrative Office (1925), p.14.

149. This was in spite of the fact that the economy was recovering by 1934.

150. Letter from the Provincial Commissioner, Kigoma Province, to the The Honourable Chief Secretary, Dar es Salaam, 1st August 1922, p.38.

the Boma. Kalulu was told that the District Commissioner would come to see what was happening but, when this commissioner failed to appear, Kalulu lost patience, took the law into his own hands and burned down the new huts. Both the missionaries and Ngomayalufu complained, and the British responded by fining Kalulu seventy East African shillings and imprisoning him at Tukuyu. Kalulu's downfall was exploited by Ngomayalufu who took control of the whole Mpimbwe territory. However, he faced continued opposition from the chief's committee (*Wakombe*) based at the chiefly headquarters at Maji Moto. They declared that Ngomayalufu could not rule over Mpimbwe whilst Kalulu (the senior hereditary chief) was still alive, and therefore withheld special chiefly equipment such as the three legged stool and *mpazi*.[151] After his release from prison, Kalulu returned to Namanyere where he was given some casual employment and died in 1966, without trying to reassert his claims to being chief.

Picture 7. The stool of the chiefs of Mpimbwe. Photo Peter Mgawe (2009).

There is no doubt that the British, as had the Germans previously, played on and magnified the conflict between Kalulu and Ngomayalufu to their own advantage during this ongoing conflict. Interestingly however they were themselves also manipulated. Willis alludes directly to,

---

151. Such equipment can today be found at Mamba and belongs to the current chief of that area, Luchensa III, who descends from chief Kalulu's side.

"references in missionary records and notes in the Sumbawanga District Book
[which] suggest that the ... authorities occasionally made use of the rivalry that
existed in their time between senior and junior members of the Pimbwe royal
family, but were also frequently used in their turn by the rival camps to further
their own interests."[152]

During this early British period the chiefly system persisted through
inheritance. After Ngomayalufu's death in 1923, a man named Zunda succeeded,
who also took the name Ngomayalufu. Zunda has been described as a "half-
wit" who was addicted to drink, and who became unpopular with nearly all the
Pimbwe.[153] Over the years it became increasingly apparent that something would
have to be done as Zunda, who was only fifteen years old when elected chief, proved
himself again and again to be totally incompetent of carrying out his duties,[154] and
was reportedly a heavy smoker of *bangi* (marijuana) which was becoming a social
problem in the area at the time. Then, on 18th October 1928, Zunda died following
a particularly heavy beer drinking session. Although some people suggested that
poisoning was involved, it proved impossible to verify this claim one way or the
other.[155] He was replaced by Kakoma, and subsequently Nsokolo II.

4.2 Village Concentrations and Underdevelopment

The 1920s and 30s in Rukwa, and much of rural Tanzania, were a turbulent time,
caused in part by the after-effects of WW1, in part by worldwide consequences
of the Great Economic Depression, and in part by the emergence of a new form
of land use, namely the alienation of tribal territories for establishing Game
Reserves for colonial hunters and early conservationists who were supported by
the International Flora and Fauna Society of London. Some characteristics of this
period can be illustrated with developments in the relationship between man and
nature in Rukwa Valley.

Traditionally, Pimbwe lived in villages and small hamlets dotted around the
wooded areas of the valley. In fact, Père Maurice's first description of Mpimbwe
in 1906 describes an area where (he estimates) 80% of the land was forested, 19%
was open plains, and 1% cleared areas for cultivation. It was in these cultivated
islands that villages were situated.[156] The burning, clearing and cultivating of fields

152. Willis (1966), p.54.

153. Letter from the Provincial Commissioner, Kigoma Province to The Honourable Chief Secretary, Dar es
Salaam, 1st August 1922, p.38.

154. Père Maurice (1935), p.242.

155. Letter from the Provincial Commissioner, Kigoma Province to The Honourable Chief Secretary, Dar es
Salaam, 1st August 1922, p.39.

156. Père Maurice (1935), p.22.

around the villages will have kept at bay the tsetse flies, and the accompanying sleeping sickness disease that can be deadly to humans.[157] However, at the end of the 19th century, a number of factors combined to upset this apparent balance of humans and nature.

First, as we have already described, the human population was greatly reduced, in part because of mortality in the Small Wars and WWI, and in part because of labour out-migration. Second, much less land was in production, because of both the declining male labour force and a British Ordinance that banned Pimbwe's customary practice of burning land before cultivation. Third, the British, under the same Ordinance, put huge areas of forest under protection in line with colonial interests in sport hunting and game conservation.

All of these factors led to abandoned land reverting to bush, and this sparked a surge in tsetse flies and sleeping sickness, exacerbated by a resurgence in the numbers of wildlife now recovering from the rinderpest epidemic of the late 19th century. Sleeping sickness became so prevalent that the British closed the road to Tabora, trying to contain the epidemic, and in the same year Ufipa District was quarantined and closed to labour recruiters, with the exception of those Africans who had already entered into pre-existing contracts.[158] The British turned to more desperate measures, deciding to directly remove people away from the increasingly forested and tsetse-ridden areas. It was under these circumstances that a campaign was launched in 1927 to relocate great numbers of people from the remoter bush areas of the Rukwa Valley (see Map 3).[159] People hated this policy because they were often forcibly removed from their homes – chased out by the police or the army if they did not go voluntarily – and with no compensation.[160] The last palisaded fortresses were now abandoned. One effect of this removal was that many Pimbwe lost their ties to much of their traditional realm, and to some of the places that feature in their origin myths. Another was that it diminished man's control of the natural environment and led to huge swathes of traditional Pimbwe territory reverting to tsetse-infested bush land.[161]

---

157. Tsetse flies need the blood of animals and the shade of trees to survive, so avoid clearings disturbed by humans.

158. Ufipa District Annual Report (1925), p.3 & 8.

159. Examples of settlements where people were removed from include Mongwe, and all the old villages shown in the Old Villages of Mpimbwe (1927) map.

160. Oral interview with Daniel Kasike (July 2011).

161. Tambila (1981), p.240.

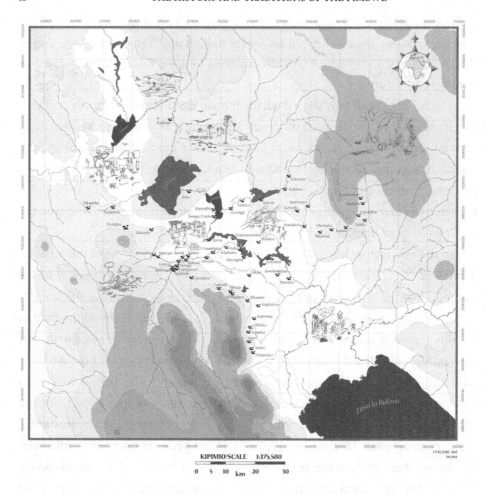

KIPIMIO/SCALE   1:375,580

0   5   10   km   20   30

Map 3. The villages of Mpimbwe in 1927.

The village concentrations of 1927 were driven by not only the motivation to protect people from tsetse flies, but also to establish centres for promoting agricultural development, schools, health facilities, commerce and religion. However there was also an important political dimension. The District Commissioner of the period felt that the area was at this time "passing through a period of transition" and that "the main aim and object of the Administration [was] tribal reorganization."[162] The Administration aimed to achieve these two objectives simultaneously, as the following quote demonstrates,

> *"It has been found necessary in order to combat the spread of the disease to make large concentrations of the people, and the groupings are so made that they may in each case form the nucleus of a newly organized tribal community."*[163]

162. Ufipa District Annual Report (1925), p.3.

163. Ufipa District Annual Report (1925), p.4.

Although it is difficult to reach any definitive conclusions because of a lack of material, it seems quite likely that the British concentration policy was as much concerned with reducing the power of petty chiefs, interlopers and usurpers in remote areas, as it was with introducing basic education and health facilities or banishing the tsetse fly.

It is said that by this time Mpimbwe (consisting of large villages such as Usevya, Mamba, Kakuni (present day Kibaoni) and Manga had 9,800 people, and was one of the largest tribal "concentrations" in the area; other ethnic groups were settled at Inyonga, Ilunde, Urawila and Rungwa. The concentrated settlements nevertheless proved to be a failure as far as they intensified economic stagnation. People found their new villages had become "islands in a sea of tsetse."[164] They felt more cut off from the rest of the country than ever, and trading opportunities were further diminished because of the ecological controls that had been put in place.

Even when the bans were ultimately lifted, cash crops like rice, groundnuts and maize failed because of improper land use, inadequate transport to export the goods, and an absence of any processing technology, such as a ginnery or oil press. Furthermore, famine became, yet again, a major problem, the result of lack of rain, overgrazing, soil exhaustion, and soil erosion. Overgrazing and soil degradation were themselves caused in part because of the higher densities of people cultivating in the new village concentrations, in part because these new villages were not always well situated for agriculture, in part because too few nitrogen-enriching crops like beans were planted, and in part because too much coracan (African finger millet, planted for beer brewing) was inter-planted with maize and exhausted the nutrients in the soil.[165]

Land alienation for external commercial purposes, which might have stimulated the local economy, was also very limited in Rukwa. Two German prospectors surveyed the area in 1927, but nothing came of this (with the exception of small trading posts). A British settler, George Damm, attempted to trade cattle, but evidently resorted to the use of force and had only limited success. Disease was also rife, such as in Usevya which endured a rat plague in 1927 at the time of the tsetse resettlement and around 200 cases of venereal disease in 1934.[166]

The economic difficulties plagued not only Rukwa but the whole world, as this was the time of the Great Depression. There was less work on the coastal and northern plantations, such that even by the late 1930s district figures suggest that penetration of the money economy into the region was still poor, with the exception of tax payments in most areas.[167] Lake Tanganyika was successful

---

164. Kjekshus, (1977), p.163. Kjekshus compares two maps, one in 1913 and the other in 1937 which show the extent of the tsetse fly belts and reveal that, whereas in 1913 the front extended as far as a line drawn from Karema eastwards roughly to the Tabora longitude and then southwards to the east of Lake Rukwa, the 1937 map leaves only the Ufipa plateau free.

165. Tambila (1981), p.244.

166. Tambila (1981), p.234-5.

167. Areas previously under Belgian control were released from tax for a year in 1921 because they had been treated so harshly and were in revolt. The boundary between the Belgian and British-controlled areas was between Mpanda and Pimbwe.

in producing *dagaa* (a small sardine-like fish, Kiswahili) but inhabitants of Mpimbwe had to make long treks to Ujiji, Uvinza or Tabora to collect it from markets or depots, and therefore profits were minimal. All of the above factors stimulated further desperate emigration, as did the constant threat of new tax hikes. Several far-sighted District Commissioners recognized the economic problems caused by the concentration policy, but could do nothing to ameliorate the outcomes. Individual men or whole families left the new villages, to look for work or a new place to live. Interestingly, many Pimbwe moved permanently to areas such as Tabora or Ubende where rural concentration settlement policies were not practiced. In short, as we move into the 1940s, we find Rukwa still to be an underdeveloped labour reserve.[168]

It was only after World War II that the British in East Africa turned to planning more ambitious, large scale development projects in rural areas – these included schemes for producing peanuts, rice, tobacco, cotton and cattle across many of the remoter parts of the country. Naturally, mechanization was integral to these new initiatives, but for the most part these projects failed and were not popular. In fact, part of the reason for helping to understand the rise and success of TANU (Tanzanian African National Union, which ultimately became responsible for Independence) in the countryside at this time was the widespread popular resentment against colonial agricultural policy.

These schemes did not reach Rukwa for two reasons. First, given its peripheral location it had a long-standing reputation of being of marginal significance. As has been already mentioned the whole of it had – as early as 1910 – earned the epithet of that "forgotten corner" of German East Africa. In 1913 Rukwa was considered a military district, of strategic importance in the upcoming struggle among the British, Belgium and Germans, but with little apparent productive power or infrastructure that could be harnessed by the colonial/imperialist powers (other than ivory). As Tambila notes, the region was in 1914 seen as rather out of the way regarding communications, leading to his suggestion that "such remoteness was then used as an excuse for continued neglect."[169] In the 1930s British officials still referred to the zone as a "wilderness". However there was a second reason for this lack of investment in Rukwa – it was (as we have already seen) a useful source of labour for other parts of Tanganyika. Accordingly, the lack of capital investment, the concentration policies, and the taxes all enmeshed people in a net of poverty. Rukwa was therefore not backward because it was outside the modern economy, but rather because the modern economy kept it outside.

---

168. Tambila (1981), p.202.

169. Tambila (1981), p.265.

CHAPTER FIVE

CULTURE AND TRADITIONS

In this chapter we discuss traditional practices in Mpimbwe, usually with a past tense. However many practices and beliefs persist to this day, albeit in a different form. Contemporary Mpimbwe since Independence is the subject of the final chapter.

5.1 Chiefs

In the past, chiefs (*mwene*) were greatly revered individuals, treated with huge respect at least among certain sections of society. It was their role to preserve the customs and traditions of the Pimbwe. They made decisions on behalf of the whole tribe and were frequently sought for advice. The position of chief was both inherited and dependent on selection by the chiefly committee (*wakombe*). This was a powerful body of men who helped the chief to rule but who were very much under his administrative command. It included such men as the *Mwene wakandawe* (the chief's gatekeeper), the *Mwene widumbi* (the 'father' of the chief who washed the chief's feet and also took charge of the administration of his dominion), the *Mwene wakuling'anga* (the person who made special medicines to protect the chief against witchcraft), the *Mwene mgabhe* (the chief's personal secretary elected by the elders) and the *Mwene wakatakwi* who was in charge of the chief's medical health. As noted earlier, the Pimbwe territory was divided into governing districts to facilitate supervision of different management activities. These districts were known as *ivikandawa* and those in charge of them were sub-chiefs called *Mwene nkandawa*, meaning they were representatives of the chief, and could themselves become locally powerful.[170]

The authority of the Pimbwe chiefs, weaker than those of their Fipa neighbours, was based on both descent and the claim to magical powers. They gained their status from their abilities to influence rain, the occurrence of natural disasters and the outcomes of war. In this sense, the magical paraphernalia of the chief, such as his stool, gourds and drums, were very important; two particularly important drums, called Nsokolo (1.50m high) and Akamalala (0.5m high), were used to confer legitimacy at his inauguration. The chief also had the right to enforce trials by poison. This was a supernatural way of deciding where human judgment failed, as far as wrongdoers would die from the poison whereas the innocent would vomit.[171] Chiefs were accordingly viewed as semi-deities – adored, feared and sometimes loathed. They also had rights to take tribute from their subjects. The main thing

---

170. Willis (1966), p.55 and oral interview with Pigangoma (July 2011).
171. Tambila (1981), p.62.

they extracted from people was foodstuffs, and they would insist that a portion of all harvests came to them even if they were not in need, simply to demonstrate power and perhaps ensure redistribution. They also took knives, hoes, fish traps and ivory from their subjects, as well as directly imposing fines.[172] They had no permanent armies, but as we have seen, could summon *ruga-ruga*. Some chiefs had special hunting and fishing reserves set aside just for their use; others had harems of up to twenty wives, and could demand women (even married women) at their will.[173] Some were also know to take their subjects as slaves and sell them to a trader.[174]

Picture 8. Drum in chief's house in Usevya. Photo Monique Borgerhoff Mulder (2010).

Chiefly inheritance was matrilineal, passing from the mother's brother to the sister's son. A chief was inaugurated by being smeared with lion's oil and – unless the unfolding of events dictated otherwise – he would continue to rule until his death. When a chief became ill, no one was allowed to see him. It was an extremely secretive time, possibly because of inheritance concerns, or otherwise because people feared that their children could be used as part of the burial process. This is because, one story goes, once a chief had died, two young children were buried alive at the head and feet of the chief to act as a "*msamilo*" or pillow for him; another account tells that a chief is buried with a male slave under his head and

---

172. Oral interview with Padre Mwiga (July 2011).

173. Père Maurice (1935), p.230-231.

174. Père Maurice (1935), p.231.

his favourite wife under his feet.[175] Yet, other accounts state that it was customary for the chief to be buried whilst seated on a three-legged 'chiefly' stool. Although we cannot verify the truth of whether young children, or anyone else, were buried alive together with the chief in the past, all contemporary Pimbwe people are aware of the story which suggests there must have been widespread fear of chiefly burials.[176] Indeed Père Maurice, in his account of the chiefs of Mpimbwe, reports that after the death of Mfundo in 1908, the chief's wife was so fearful for her life that she sought refuge in the Catholic mission.

The period of the death of the chief was known as *Iyulu Lyatela* meaning "the country has grown teeth." Strictly, at the death of a chief, no one was allowed to cry. The only people present at the burial were the chief's committee and other important individuals. Chiefs had their own private burial ground on the side of Lake Chada both before (and possibly after) Katavi became a National Park. After the National Park was established, and following the split of the Pimbwe territory into two chiefly realms (as accounted above), the burial was conducted either alongside the river Kavuu at Iteme for Usevya chiefs, or (for the deceased chiefs of Mamba) at a place called *Kuli Masigo* or *Musyigo*, the Nyamwezi term for royal tombs, near to the hot spring at Maji Moto. This allowed for their bodies to be washed away when the rains came which was particularly important to prevent traditional doctors and wild animal hunters exhuming the bodies to make protective medicines (*kizimba*). Food and alcohol were taken to the burial ceremony. Elders from the chief's committee slaughtered one chicken and one goat as relish, and the blood was used in an offering on top of the chief's grave. The remaining food left over was not allowed to be taken home, and all the utensils also had to remain at the burial site.

The people of Mpimbwe were not informed directly about the death of the chief nor, as mentioned above, allowed to cry. Sometimes a bell was rung by the *mgabhe* (the chief's assistant) as a sign of his death. Otherwise, the only way of detecting the end of the reign was that a spear would be placed point down in front of the chief's residence which indicated he had died. If the spear was directed upwards, this indicated that another chief had been nominated.

Some of the more infamous Pimbwe chiefs such as Ngomayalufu and Kalulu have already been mentioned but discussions with various older members of the Pimbwe community have revealed some observations on the lives of other chiefs who have ruled. In all, there have been twenty-five chiefs in the Pimbwe territory; the full list based on the work of Willis, can be found in Table 1.[177] It is however important to bear in mind that the order of the earlier chiefs cannot be conclusively confirmed.

---

175. Père Maurice (1935), p.233.

176. Oral interview with Daniel Kasike (July 2011).

177. Willis (1966), p.53. Note however that some variations appear in the list given to Père Maurice, a priest working in Mpimbwe at an earlier period (Père Maurice, 1935, p.239).

Picture 9. Burial place of chiefs at Kavuu river. Photo Monique Borgerhoff Mulder (2006).

Table 1: The chiefs of Mpimbwe with dates of their deaths when this is known[a]

1. Luchensa I	14. Kasogera I
2. Chondo	15. Mfundo (1902)
3. Nsokolo I	16. Kasogera I (1908) (same as 14)
4. Kutakula	17. Kalulu Mpandasyalo
5. Zumbi	18. Nsumba Ngomayalufu (1923)
6. Kamfawa	19. Zunda Ngomayalufu
7. Luchensa II	20. Kakoma
8. Katambala Kifyenko	21. Nsokolo II (1944)
9. Katandala [b]	22. Kaninsya Bonifasi
10. Ilumba	23. Thadeo Ngomayalufu II (2003)
11. Bembu Lyoba	24. John Kalele Zunda (2011)[c]
12. Nsumba	25. Luchensa III (Edes Malaso)[d]
13. Singa	

a The list differs somewhat from that of the french priest Père Maurice, published in 1935, p239: 1) Nsokolo, 2) Katambala, 3) Chondo, 4) Zumbi, 5) Kamfwa, 6) Lukensa, 7) Katambala, 8) Katanda, 9) Ilumba, 10) Bembu, 11) Sumba, 12) Singa, 13) Kasagela, 14) Fundo, 15) Nsokolo
b This and the three following chiefs only had very short administrations
c A successor has not yet been chosen
d The current chief of Mamba

We do of course know that Chondo took over power after Luchensa died, a rightful inheritance because in some origin stories he was the son of Luchensa's sister, Mtembozi. The next chief was known as Nsokolo I, he is thought to have made the magic three-legged stool (which still exists to this day with Luchensa III). There is some doubt as to the exact line of chieftainship after Nsokolo's rule, but what is known is that these chiefs ruled against the backdrop of an ongoing war between the Mpimbwe and the Bende (the latter of whom were also known as the Sowa). The Bende were ambitious to expand their territory, and Chief Katambala Kifyenko fought fiercely with the Bende to restore the Pimbwe realm. He was successful in this task.

Katambala may have been brave but he was also said to have been disrespectful to the queen-mother, Mwasi Mankoma, who was highly regarded. It was for this reason that the *Wakombe* removed him from power, although this did not relieve the tension since it was generally believed that Mwasi Mankoma had cursed all of Katambala's successors owing to his dismissive behaviour towards her. This fraught situation created what is said to be one of the most difficult moments ever experienced in the Mpimbwe chiefdom. Meanwhile the Bende invasions resumed, whilst the Konongo and the Bungu had also both infiltrated the Rukwa Valley. Under the reign of Chief Ilumba, the Bende retook control of Mpimbwe and retained control for some time, causing Ilumba to eventually run away. Later on, as the story goes, a power vacuum ensued after Mwasi Mankoma had no more sons to become chief, the validity of which is supported both by the suggestion that Katambala had no clear heir and by the report that Ilumba, Bembu, Nsumba and Singa only had very short reigns.[178] As a result, Kasogera was appointed by the Cabinet to take up the chieftaincy despite opposition from some elders who complained that he did not belong to the correct line of the chiefly family, as we have seen. In fact, Kasogera was said to be a common man who was a low-status potter working for Mwasi Mankoma. During the early years of his administration, Kasogera fought with the Konongo and won the war. Yet, despite his victory, opposition to him crystallized because of his lack of legitimacy to the chieftaincy and he was deposed by chief Mfundo as we recounted.[179] Kasogera went to live with the Fipa chief, Kimalaunga, at a place named Isagalilo (the story of Kasogera and his ensuing conflict with Mfundo has already been told earlier).

Kasogera's death precipitated a succession crisis. The chief's council removed

---

178. Père Maurice (1935), p.239.

179. Although running contrary to Willis' list of chiefs, this is one school of thought which appears to be quite credible.

all power from his family, decreeing that they had no legitimate right to the chieftainship. Instead, they turned power to the real chief's line, awarding it to Kalulu who at the time was living with his mother at a place called Churangwa, lying south of Mlele in Ugongwe and north of the Ngolima River. Meanwhile, the small chiefdom wing left by Kasogera did not accept the idea of the chief's council stripping power from them and awarding it to Kalulu. In response, they used force to elect Nsumba Mwananyima, who was a grandson of Kasogera, and who inherited the name of Ngomayalufu. The on-going conflict that consequently erupted between Ngomayalufu and Kalulu has been covered in much detail already. Kalulu's first spell in jail (for ordering the missionary priests to be whipped) allowed Ngomayalufu to obtain a stranglehold on the Pimbwe territory which Kalulu greatly objected to upon leaving jail. He claimed that he had been stripped of his rightful title. In an attempt to bring consensus to both sides, the Germans divided Mpimbwe into two parts, Usevya and Mamba around 1900. This division still exists to this day under the recently deceased chief John Kalele Zunda (of Usevya) and Luchensa III (of Mamba). After Kalulu was released from jail the second time (having served eleven years for burning down Mbede village), the country had become independent and chiefly power was greatly reduced (as we will see later). It is interesting that Kalulu now asked the missionaries to baptize him, highly ironic given all his skirmishes with them previously. He died a Christian in 1966.

Picture 10. Burial place of chiefs at Maji Moto. Photo Monique Borgerhoff Mulder (2010).

5.2 Traditional Customs and Livelihoods

Population and Social Organization

The earliest count of the Pimbwe was made in 1931, at 4999 souls[180], somewhat smaller than Père Maurice's earlier estimate of 6000 people living in an area of 4000 km².[181] At the 1948 census, they were 13,137, but by 1957 had strangely decreased to 11,479. As described earlier, Pimbwe lived in villages and hamlets. These were formed into administrative districts (*ivikandawa*), under the authority of the sub-chief (*Mwene nkandawa*) and village headman (*basengi*).

Pimbwe were loosely recognized as either belonging to the royal line (*Batembezi* or *Abantu ya Kawe*) or as commoners (*Bakapimbwe*). They were also organized into clans (*uluko*), with a perpetual alternation of two *uluko* names in each patrilineage, such that a man or woman shares *uluko* membership with his or her grandchildren and grandparents.[182] *Uluko* membership did not preclude marriage, conveyed some idea of shared ancestry, and was typically associated with a totemic animal that could not be eaten.[183] While the rules of succession go from a man to his sister's son in the chiefly lineage, among commoners children are tightly linked both to their fathers and their mother's brothers.

Material Culture

The Pimbwe used to live in round houses (*duara*) with conical roofs made using sticks covered with mud and thatched grass. They were often also surrounded by a wall made of grass (*ulukutu*). Houses later became typically rectangular, after the Pimbwe supposedly saw and copied this type of house from Tabora during their period of ivory trading with the Nyamwezi.

Clothing tended to be made from *ikipuka*, a cloth made of animal skins.[184] Men traditionally wore reedbuck and bushbuck whilst women wore goatskins. In terms of crafts, various handcraft activities were carried out such as weaving mats made from palm leaves (*masandalala*), creating baskets made from reeds which grew along the riverbank, and making trowels, mortars and pestles from local wood sources.

As tribal marks men and women had the two lower incisors removed at puberty, and both sexes shaved their heads.

Agriculture, Hunting and Food

In previous times, as we noted before, much of the Pimbwe land was covered

---

180. Willis (1966), p.53.

181. Père Maurice (1935), p.30.

182. Willis (1966), p.55.

183. Père Maurice (1938) La Géographie, LXX Le Pays des Bapimbwe, p.88.

184. Père Maurice (1937), p.233.

with natural vegetation. Elders say that this was due to the existence of more plentiful rainfall than nowadays, but without data on rainfall patterns in the past, this cannot be confirmed; certainly, Mpimbwe was much more forested than it is nowadays. Rainfall was and is of course crucial to the livelihoods of the Pimbwe people (not just for drinking, cooking and washing, but also for building mud houses), and ensuring its reliability has been a major concern of Pimbwe cosmology, particularly the role of the god Katavi. Rain allowed both the rivers Kavuu and Msadya to flow with water throughout the year, providing for plenty of fish, a central element of the Pimbwe diet. The land was fertile enough that crop cultivation did not require the application of fertilizers. People used a scratch hoe to cultivate the land, and seeds were obtained from the farms of their neighbours as well as locations as distant as Lyangalile, the center of Ufipa.[185]

Staple food crops grown were finger millet (to make *ubhugali* porridge), (or to brew alcohol), simsim, sweet potatoes (popular types were and still are *kandolo* and *milambo*), and groundnuts; pumpkins and small tomatoes grew interspersed with planted crops in the fields. Maize was probably first introduced in the 18th century, and is also used to make *ubhugali*. Cassava is a very important crop for providing food security in periods of drought, and sweet potatoes were sliced and dried in the sun to store for the hunger season. Tobacco was grown on the edges of the village. In many parts of Mpimbwe cultivation was facilitated by building ridges enriched with organic matter and ash.[186] The definition of laziness in Mpimbwe was someone who did not care for his or her farm, and unlike many Bantu communities, men as well as women were expected to do farm work.[187] Nevertheless, there was a joke that the Pimbwe used to tie the wings of roosters so that they would not be woken by their calls early in the morning.

Families would spend the agricultural season living by their fields, beating pans and drums at night to frighten off wild animals. Seedlings needed to be protected against birds, and ripening crops from bushpigs, elephants, monkeys and baboons. Locusts were another major source of crop loss, causing a serious famine in 1926.[188] Much attention was paid to crop storage. Solid wall bins and open timber platforms (*intarita*) were constructed to keep pests out. A traditional pesticide of ashes, pepper and tobacco was made to ward off infestations by beetles and other insects. Indeed, some families still use this method today because it is cheap. Seeds for crops such as groundnuts were stored in big jars and covered with earth on top (*ukumatilila*) so as to prevent bugs or children from eating

185. Oral interview with Pimbwe farmer Victor Kalelembe from Manga village (2008).
186. Willis (1966), p.58.
187. Père Maurice (1937), p.147.
188. Père Maurice (1937), p.157.

them. Similarly, seeds for beans were mixed with ashes and the dry waste of an animal such as a chicken or a duck to prevent an insect attack.

Agricultural produce was supplemented with wild foods (game meat like buffalo and impala, fish and bush vegetables) as well as by domestic goats, chickens and ducks. Eland and zebra were particularly favoured for their fattiness, and some species were tabooed as a result of clan membership. Pimbwe did not own cattle because it was too labour intensive for them to herd the animals. To this day, Pimbwe are not keen to keep cattle. It appears that there was some variability in the amount of food produced each year which, certainly in relation to crop production, was probably heavily dependent upon the weather. Undoubtedly years of plenty were interspersed with years of scarcity, as in much of Africa. During these dry years bush foods, including honey, wild fruits, wild grains, tubers and grasshoppers were critical; indeed, in any year honey was considered a delicacy, and many Pimbwe specialized in its production.[189]

Picture 11. Hunting opportunities at Ikuu. Photo Tim Caro (2010).

To be short of food was considered embarrassing, unless this was due to a family member being sick, or a death; people seen as "lazy" were apparently often shunned by other members of the community. In cases of severe food shortfalls, a household would seek help from relatives, or work for unrelated households and receive payment in grain.[190]

Madimu, the treasured food of the Pimbwe and central to their cultural identity,

---

189. Père Maurice (1937), p.159.

190. Père Maurice (1937), p.158.

remains a particular delicacy to this day. *Madimu* are very large beetle larvae that hatch from eggs laid by females inside the *Mgunga* tree, traditionally cut down for firewood. *Madimu* are rich in fat and Pimbwe people say that they would prefer to be deprived of meat than *madimu*. Unfortunately, this Pimbwe speciality has become a rare commodity, as it is increasingly difficult to find *Mgunga* trees outside Katavi National Park. The establishment of the National Park means that it is illegal for people to harvest *madimu*. It is possible to obtain a license for access to the park, but these are very expensive and the average Pimbwe person is unsure how the process works.

Picture 12. Large larvae (madimu) favoured as a delicacy by Pimbwe. Photo Tim Caro (2008).

It is clear that the traditional settlements (see Map 3) of the Pimbwe people were inside what is now Katavi National Park between Mongwe in the west and the Mlele mountains in the east. These villagers lived in close proximity to wild animals and supplemented their cultivation with a great deal of hunting and fishing. Evidence of this can been seen from the grinding stones and potsherds which are still found in the park to this day. Game was plentiful, and hunting was central to the Pimbwe way of life in those days, and important to the Pimbwe identity. For example, if a male youth ate vegetables, it pointed to fear and laziness on his part because he was not prepared to go hunting and, as a result, he would have struggled to find a wife.

There are various inconsistent reports about different animals being taboo, such as giraffe, zebra and hippopotamus. Behind this logic lay a superstitious fear that anyone who ate their meat would be afflicted in some unfortunate way. For example, eating meat from a hippopotamus was believed to lead to contracting leprosy, or giving birth to a child with leprosy. It seems most likely however that these taboos were specific to different clans.[191] Although perhaps not intentional, these taboos may have resulted in the conservation of some of these wild animals.

Picture 13. Grinding stone found in Katavi National Park. Photo Aditya Swami (2010).

Hunting took place in both the dry and rainy seasons and involved the use of dogs, spears, bow and arrows, traps and nets; according to which particular animal was being hunted. In fact the Pimbwe were remarkably ingenious with trapping, their use of dogs, and their ambushing animals with fire; they made special ingenious devices for catching different animals, such as self-closing cages for antelope and huge concealed pits for elephants with upturned spears lining the bottom; they were also apparently very brave in scavenging from lions.[192] The arrival of traders from the coast introduced muzzleloader guns (*ingoho*) to the region, weapons that have been passed down from one generation to the next. Apart from the killing of elephants for their ivory, hunting was not a commercial enterprise. Men killed to obtain food and the meat was brought back to the village. Evidence from an archaeological excavation at Kibaoni, the ancient village site of Kakuni, indicates that impala, buffalo, warthogs, bushpigs, and giraffe were

191. Willis (1966), p.55.

192. Père Maurice (1937) Le Pays des Bapimbwe (suite) LXVII, p.219.

commonly eaten, in conjunction with protein from goats.[193] Some reports claim that meat was divided equally amongst families who would eat collectively at the ibhanja (discussed below), others that most cooking occurred within families.

Fishing was also central to the Pimbwe way of life (although perhaps less so than to their neighbours, the Rungwa). Fishing became increasingly important as each year the level of the rivers began to fall. The main fishing sites were on the Msadya and Kavuu rivers, where catfish (*ikambale*) are numerous. Fishermen avoided Lake Rukwa because of the crocodiles. Young men would use fishing lines, hooks, traps and baskets, often building weirs as the rivers drained, in which to trap the remaining fish. There are also reports of strange jumping fish that would leap up waterfalls, and be caught (with four sided hooks) in the smooth upper pools. Fishing, like game hunting, was both a collective and an individual activity, and part of the harvest was supposed to be given to the chief.

Picture 14. Fishing weir (Kibaoni village,). Photo Craig Hadley (2004).

This topic cannot be left without a few words on beer, of which the Pimbwe were very fond, particularly in the dry season when there was no pressing agricultural work. Beer was made through a fermentation process of maize and millet.[194] Respected families were expected to host at least two or three beer parties a year, to which people would come from over twenty miles, and which would gain the hosts considerable status. Usually these were jolly affairs, but sometimes ended in violence. Tobacco use, probably adopted from Arab traders and grown in plots close to the village, was also popular. Both men and women enjoyed tobacco, both

193. Foutch et al. (2009), p.262

194. Père Maurice (1937), p. 209.

in pipes and as snuff. Marijuana use was also reported as popular in the 1930s.[195]

Birth, Growing Up and Marriage

When a woman went into labour, her husband would call a midwife (*malombwe* or *nakambusa*) who brought several older women to assist her. They would light a fire in the hut to be kept burning continuously until they left, and would also receive help from the woman's mother and mother-in-law or rub the woman's belly with warm water. Whilst it was the husband's duty to supply firewood, neither he nor any other man was permitted to enter the hut whilst the midwives were there. Pregnant women were given incisions into which the powder of various roots and leaves were rubbed. If the birth was difficult or slow, advice was sought from diviners (*mfumu*) to find the cause. If the woman cried out in pain she was chided by the mother and mother-in-law. The afterbirth was buried in the hut by the bed.[196] The umbilical cord (*ubukala*) was not cut but instead tied to the newborn's abdomen until it later fell off; a midwife then hid it in the fork of a tree.[197] After the birth, the fire was put out and the midwives left after being paid by the husband. Newborns were fed solids, typically a mix of water and flour, and sometimes also chopped grubs (*madimu*)[198] almost immediately, because Pimbwe believed mother's milk was not enough; children were usually weaned after two years.

The arrival of twins (*amapasa*) was considered to be both a cause for fear (as potential hostile divinities) and a great blessing. Accordingly, the wider community both yelled taunts of shame at the mother at the same time as granting her great respect for giving birth to twins.[199] Traditionally, both children were placed in a winnowing basket (*ulupe*) and taken to a place where rubbish was thrown, or to a road junction, where special songs were sung. A typical song would be along the lines of:

Nyiguleli kulibhampasa ni mtundaee, mwanyimile inyama ni sumo mwalilya.[200]

Some stories recount that the parents' heads were shaved using a special alcohol (*inzubhi ya mapasa*) before being anointed with flour. The midwives then made a particular kind of porridge (*ilombo*) which was drunk by the whole family to ward off any form of fit.[201] People also performed offerings at the end of each month as a blessing for the twins (*ukusasa lwanga*). If one twin died, then the

---

195. Père Maurice (1937), p. 212.

196. Père Maurice (1935), p.310.

197. Taken from Willis (1966), p.55-56. It was considered very important that the cord did not come into contact with the newborn's genitalia because it was feared this would then cause the baby to become sterile.

198. Père Maurice (1937), p.160.

199. Père Maurice (1935), p.314.

200. This untranslatable verse requested spirits to protect twins.

201. The Pimbwe traditionally conferred much respect on midwives. They used various traditional medicines to enable women to deliver safely and were considered to be great saviours to many who were living in an area without health services. Midwives also sang songs to boost the morale of the mother during childbirth, as is written about below.

surviving twin was traditionally smeared on the head with flour and laid in the grave intended for the deceased. It was then pulled out before the deceased was buried. If both twins died, then they were buried in their own little cemetery called *kuli mapasa* ("the place of the twins").

By 6-8 years old children became semi-independent apart from relying on their parents for food. Young boys would tend their father's goats (if he had any), shoot birds, and fish in the river. Père Maurice, perhaps reflecting his missionary perspective, emphasizes the unruly behaviour among boys at puberty including stealing, lack of scruples, and lying. Little girls however are reported as playing mother's games (carrying around toy babies – a stick, gourd or corn cob), and imitating their mother's grinding of millet and other grains.[202] There were no ceremonies for reaching puberty for either sex. Girls were expected to marry soon after reaching 12 years of age, boys at between 16 and 20, and when they have identified a bride they employ a go-between (*kikwantemo*) who starts the bride price (*insabho*) negotiations, which traditionally consisted of gifts of hoes, goats, chickens, cotton and ritual items. We discuss the marriage ceremony in more detail below.

Husbands and wives traditionally never ate together, nor even talked together publicly, at least as reported Père Maurice,[203] although we have not heard that elsewhere. Their relationship was nevertheless generally one of economic cooperation, with men and women sharing farm work, men hunting and fishing, and women doing most of the domestic tasks (although men played a big role in firewood collection). The production of children was critical. Children were adored when small, but attracted much less passion once a younger sibling had been born. If the couple had no children after two years, a diviner was consulted to determine if they had been bewitched, and if so how to treat such a spell. If treatment failed, the bride usually returned to her natal home and the bride price was returned.[204]

The institution of marriage, in Père Maurice's view, seem to have been quite flimsy, with divorces potentially initiated by either a husband or wife. Others suggest divorce was difficult, even not permitted at all. In order to be divorced, it appears that the elders took charge of proceedings and the wife had to return to her father with the calabash of oil (*intuungu*) which she had taken with her upon marriage, accompanied by her husband who took his bow and arrow. The bride price had to be returned if she had no children (or if she took the children with her); should she return to her husband, he would have to pay more bride price. Her husband would also only accept her back if she returned with the calabash of oil.[205]

---

202. Père Maurice (1936) La Géographie LXVI Les pays des Bapimbwe. LXVI, p.171.

203. Père Maurice (1936), p.182.

204. Père Maurice (1936), p.183.

205. Willis (1966), p.57.

Unstable marriages, as reported by Père Maurice, may reflect the period when Rukwa was a labour reserve (i.e. 1910-1960s), when so many men were absent. It is nevertheless clear that marriage was a relationship fraught with tension. If, for example, a wife chose to return to her natal family after the death of her husband she was typically accused of having killed him through use of witchcraft; furthermore, cases of infidelity seem to have been rather common. Infidelity in women did not necessarily lead to divorce unless the woman failed to name her lover (because in this case the adulterer could not be fined), but it did add friction to the relationship, as did men's adultery (which was also common). Polygyny was the rule for chiefs, but rarer amongst commoners. Relationships among in-laws were formal, with a very respectful distance maintained between young couples and their in-laws which persisted throughout life.[206]

The Marital Ceremony

In identifying a future partner, both a man and a woman would look for someone who was not idle, enjoyed working, and whose lineage had no inheritable diseases such as leprosy or infertility, and who was not related by blood. When a man identified a potential suitor to be his wife, he sent over a *kikwantemo* (go-between) to the girl's parents who would ideally be a wise, respected person – sometimes either the father or uncle of the man who wished to marry. This man would visit early in the morning and say words to the effect of "So-and-so sent me to request for drinking water" which was a symbolic way of saying that there was a man who wished to marry their daughter. Sometimes a formal letter of engagement was also submitted. After the *kikwantemo* had left, the parents of the girl called her maternal grandmother to come and ask her if she knew the man in question and, if she did, and if the family had no objections to his situation or health, she will then agree to the marriage. The bride price was then arranged, with the *kikwantemo* acting as mediator. After it had been settled, a hoe known as *inkoma lwiye* was given as a first gift, meaning "that with which one knocks on the door"[207] (It was used for knocking at the door of the future in-laws house.) Other gifts typically included *tukolokoto*, a type of iron bracelet worn around the arm, and *vikunga* which was a goat's rope (the amount of rope depended on the amount of goats which had been given).

On the eve of the bride's wedding, she ran away from home and had to be sometimes forceably returned. Then a ritual called *ukumzovya* took place where the girl was painted with ashes and mud, with some accounts even suggesting that she was beaten. Later on, one of her brother-in-laws or another relation

---

206. Père Maurice (1936), p. 186.
207. Willis (1966), p.56.

would carry her on his back to visit the hut of her father's elder brother. This was a symbolic way of saying goodbye to the girl before she left her own family and became united with another one. When the celebrations were due to begin, people went to dig up soil whilst singing ululations. To herald this activity the bride's aunt (father's sister) would strike together an axe-blade and the head of a hoe, making a sound called *inceence*. Dancing then began and the bride was anointed with white chalk (*intakaso*).

Picture 15. Dancing at a wedding (Mirumba village). Photo Monique Borgerhoff Mulder (2008).

At three o'clock in the morning, the father's sister of the bride would boil hot water and wash the bride with the help of the bride's mother. Millet porridge was then made in the bride's hut and the groom was allowed to enter. In a ritual called *akasondya*, the groom placed some porridge in the bride's mouth and she spat it out before the bride repeated the same process to the groom. The guests then began to eat and dance whilst the bride and groom decorated themselves. She wore a dress called *amandingi* from her waist to her feet, a string of beads around her waist and two more strings crossing diagonally between her breasts. Her whole body was also anointed with oil. Her hair was then delicately plaited and decorated with traditional leaves. Special beads were also prepared which the bride wore both in her hair and around her neck. Both the groom and his escort (*icinsindi*) returned to the groom's hut, rubbed themselves with oil and decorated themselves with beads. Both the groom and the bride put an *impazi* (a white ocean sea-shell)[208] on their forehead and a *chomeka* (the feather of a multi-coloured bird called an *inkulukulu*) in their hair. The groom also carried a bow and arrow (*ubhuta*), either to fend off potential 'suitors' for his wife or to protect himself.[209]

When the bride was ready, her father permitted her to go outside and meet her husband who was waiting for her at the hut door, leaning on a staff called *intuba lya lubazi*. The bride's father would then sometimes sing to his wife,

Nyina mwana fumu sunde wapokela mali eeh! Wapokela mali eeh!
Washala mwikongo eeeh! Nyinamwanaaaa![210]

This was to remind the mother-of-the-bride to go outside and provide some final words to her daughter because the bride price had already been received. The bride was escorted outside by a group of women who introduced themselves to the groom and warned him to respect them. Whilst this was happening, a drum known as *itchitumba* was beaten and special songs were sung. The bride's father then dipped his two index fingers together in a pot of oil from the bride's hut and anointed the bride on her feet, the backs of her hands, her throat and the back of her neck. He repeated this process with the groom. He then instructed the groom on his responsibilities. Afterwards, soil from the bride's hut was used to anoint the couple in the same way. The role then turned to the groom's father who also anointed the couple with oil and instructed his son on his duties as a husband.

Another example of a song sung by the bride's family and friends is as follows and gives us some indication of the pride and ambition they have for their daughter,

Twavulana yashalintende, Kamala nsabho ndyamambembo nalinkanile
Kamala nsabho ndyamambembo, nalinkanile.[211]

The groom's side used singing to praise the groom for his success in winning over the woman and criticize rivals who had competed with him to marry the same person. In one well-remembered song, a rival was compared to a baboon who entered a maize farm but made every plant he touched become unripe. In contrast the groom successfully harvested one ripe maize cob from the same farm, and teases his rival for his spurned ambition.

Fulani mkunankuka wamali ntendee!
Ukufika mwintende kolola wa tonya litachilee!

---

208. This is the shell of a giant clam and they would typically have bought this from a trader.

209. Willis (1966), p.56.

210. Translation is "Mother of the daughter come out side and give your advice/last word to your daughter; You have received a bride price eeh! You have received the bride price eeeh! You have remained the mother of the daughter, eeh!"

211. The translation of this is "Many men wanted to give their money for this lady, but the parents refused because they wanted to see their daughter marry the best person possible."

Mwamnola kuminso kutimpaka siselaaaa![212]

When the ceremony itself was complete, the bride sat on the legs of her aunt who customarily sat on a three-legged stool (*kigoda*). The groom and his escort then pulled some leaves from the house of his new father-in-law to signal that the couple are now married and his daughter is leaving the family home. Later that evening, two hours after sunset, the sisters of the groom went to collect the bride and took her to the groom. It was now that the ritual of *kivi* took place, involving special money (not bride price) being given to the bride to show that she was now responsible for cooking for the family. Legend has it that it was the bride's aunt's role to collect the *kivi* and the bride would refuse to enter the groom's house until the appropriate amount had been offered by him.

The aunt also played a crucial part in proclaiming whether the bride was a virgin or not. Maintaining virginity was considered to be very important as a source of respect and pride both for the bride and her family. Prior to cohabitation, the aunt covered their bed with a white cloth. The next morning she went to the door of the newly weds and requested the cloth so that she could see if it was bloodstained or not. If it was good news, the aunt ululated to cheer for the news. The mother of the bride was then given a gift by her husband as a sign that she was the producer of 'the beautiful one' and had looked after her daughter well. If the cloth was not bloodstained, the bride's mother was rebuked for her carelessness and it is said that she was sometimes fined. Early loss of virginity brought great shame upon the family of the bride, and songs were often sung about such cases. This may well have acted as an incentive for other brides to ensure the same did not befall them.

After the bride left the family home the morning after the wedding, she went directly to her father-in-law's house with a basket of flour and a chicken. Before entering inside, a chicken or goat was slaughtered at the foot of the door. The bride would then traditionally jump over the door and enter the house whilst songs were sung such as,

Twabhonedya kabhundi mpako, njulile kawakolo.[213]

This ritual was also performed between the bride's family and their new son-in-law, the aim being to officially welcome the newcomer into the family. Whilst at her in-laws, the bride was taught household works, known as *ukumkupudya*, such as cooking and fetching water. However, she only remained there for one day before

---

212. No direct translation of this is possible, but it concerns the conflict between a groom and his rivals.

213. The literal translation is "We have got her so let her come in."

returning to her family home because superstition ruled that she should not eat food twice consecutively whilst staying there. The new bride wore a copper bracelet called an *iciteba* on her left wrist as an indication that she was now married.

Death

When an adult died hot water was poured on the head of the body, and the eyes and mouth were closed. Prior to the arrival of missionaries, the Pimbwe buried corpses in round unmarked graves, although a tree was sometimes planted as a marker.[214] These graves were small, so it was necessary for the corpse's legs to be broken so that they could sit properly in the round grave. With the missionaries came western influence, and the Pimbwe soon began burying people in a rectangular grave with a small partition at the centre (*mwanandani*). Burials differed greatly depending on the status of the deceased, and these customs tell us a great deal about the values of ancient Pimbwe society. Lepers, the insane and epileptics were left out in the bush (as we will see below), children under three months were buried under the bed in which they were conceived, twins and chiefs were the only individuals to be given a special burial spot, and only elephant killers and chiefs were not mourned for at the funeral.

Customarily, a corpse was cleaned by elders, covered with bed sheets and buried. Everyone attending the burial would throw earth into the grave, to prevent the deceased returning as an evil spirit. After the burial, villagers mourned for seven days. The reason for the lengthy mourning period was partly to allow relatives living far away to attend the final day of the funeral which was marked by the washing of hands; those who failed to attend the funeral were otherwise liable to being accused of being responsible for death, through the use of witchcraft. Women mourners wore strings of palm tree leaves around their neck, head and waist whilst the closest relatives shaved their heads. If the burial occurred during the rainy season, no farm work could be done during the subsequent seven day mourning period until a ritual involving the burning of a hoe had been performed. This involved burning various seeds on a hot hoe, after which standard farm activities could be resumed.

Two days before the washing of hands ceremony, men were invited to go to the forest to hunt in a ritual known as *ukusumba chizimu*. This was considered to be the best method of proving whether the deceased had died a natural death, or whether they had been bewitched. Dogs, spears and guns (*ingoho*) were used to hunt. If the men returned to the funeral with one or more animals, the death was judged to be a normal one but if no animal was killed then this was a bad omen. Hand washing normally took place in the Msadya River and brought the funeral

214. Père Maurice (1937), p.89.

proceedings to a close on the seventh day.[215] If the deceased was thought to have been bewitched, then the closest relatives were sometimes immersed in the water, supposedly to wash away the bad spirit.

Those who died in childbirth were buried by midwives and traditional healers while special songs were sung. The woman's dead body was not carried out using the normal door of the hut but removed from the house through a specially-cut hole. Before burying, the chief midwife cut the corpse of the unborn child from her stomach, and the infant was then buried in the innermost part of the same grave. People attending the funeral were not allowed to weep, with those carrying the dead woman to her grave in fact uttering cries of joy. This type of death was associated with evil spirits, and therefore the following night the deceased's hut was destroyed completely in order to ensure that another person would not be afflicted by a similar evil.[216]

A person with no children (male or female) was buried with a cinder (*kisunsulo*) between their legs or on their back. Meanwhile, when someone with leprosy or epilepsy died, they were taken to the banks of a river (primarily the river Kavuu) where their bodies were not buried but instead dumped in the bush, covered with thorns. The reasoning behind this was that it was felt the entire family would suffer from the same problem as the dead person if they were buried. If somebody died with a large sore or growth on a limb, it was severed from the body and buried next to it by the grave.

Between three months and a year after a death, it was the responsibility of close relatives to distribute any properties left by the deceased. This took place in an inheritance ceremony known as *ukubusya* or *ukusenda ividwalo* which, translated literally, means "to take the clothes" of the dead person.[217] An immediate issue here was the inheritance of the deceased's spirit and personal belongings – clothes, tools, cultivation plots, arrows and, in the case of married men, wives and children.[218] Much effort and tension went into choosing an inheritor in this sense, since he (it was almost always a man) cannot be a direct descendant, and was usually an uncle or brother. The chosen inheritor symbolizes his position by taking the clothes of the deceased. In reality, many people, particularly children, had very few material goods and could only really pass on clothes. Interestingly inheritors were usually in the generation above the deceased, unless the deceased

---

215. Close relatives often still wash their hands today at the end of a funeral ceremony. However, funerals do not tend to last for longer than three days and people do not necessarily go to the Msadya river to carry out the ritual of washing hands.

216. Willis (1966) 57-58.

217. Willis (1966), p.58.

218. Père Maurice (1937), p92.

was very old. Furthermore, there were strange family twists: if the deceased was a first-born child, then the father took the possessions, and the clothes might typically go to the grandparents on his side, but if the deceased was a second born, then inheritance automatically became a matrilineal affair, with the possessions passing to a mother's brother. If an adult died who owned cultivated land, this was traditionally passed down the male line.

Finally, should a husband die, the 'inheritance' of the widow was discussed by relatives who would come together and search for a wise person to take care of his widowed family. The widow had no choice in the matter, and was required to marry whomever her family decided upon. This was because any input from her in selecting a future spouse was considered by the family to be a possible sign that the two were engaged in a love affair and had conspired to kill her former husband. She therefore had to accept whatever decision was made for her. After the widow was 'inherited', it was considered crucial that the new couple have sexual intercourse that night to mark a new phase in their life after the death of her former husband. It was the role of the smallest grandson of the deceased to stoke the fire all night and to cook a chicken the next morning. That morning, the couple sat in front of the hut to be anointed with oil similar to what happens in the wedding ceremony. If a widow refused to be 'inherited', her children would still be passed to the heir that had been assigned and, if there were no children, this heir was entitled to the bride price given for her.

5.3 Songs, Community, and Education

Songs and dances were, and indeed continue to form, an important part of Pimbwe communal life. One theory put forward has been that traditional songs and dances derived much of their origin from neighbouring tribes such as the Fipa. Whilst current elders contest that this was the case, it does appear that people learned different styles and drum beats as these infiltrated from the coastal areas with the expansion of trade routes. Pimbwe workers returned from their travels to coastal plantations with reports and experience of these different cultures. This stimulated competition amongst returning groups as to who could bring back the most exciting and newest ideas. This applied not just to songs and dances, but also to other ways of life such as clothing and the plaiting or braiding of hair. Many Pimbwe were keen to learn about different ways of life and to pick up new songs and dances in a bid to "better themselves" and appear educated and cosmopolitan. Traditional songs nevertheless persisted, particularly those that stressed the importance of personal responsibility and respect. Most songs we still know today focus on marriage, an institution that was once strongly revered;

others on the importance of hard work and cooperation. For example, during colonial times the Germans were praised for cooperating over the construction of a rock bridge at a river crossing in Mirumba which had flooded almost annually,

Wapanga idalaya iyamawe ... Jeremani!
Wapanga idalaya iyamawe ... Jeremani!
Wapangi dalaya iyamawee! [219]

Songs also praise the generosity in hunters and the high regard in which chiefs were held (prior to their influence waning). When a chief was travelling around the local region making visits, he was carried by porters and slaves on a dais (palanquin) because there was no other means of transport suitable to his high status, a sight witnessed by some surviving elders in Mpimbwe, including M.K.P. Pinda. Songs such as,

Tusendile mwene tukalele kulichala! [220]

were sung to give motivation and encouragement to the porters whilst they carried their master.

Midwives also sang songs during childbirth which gives an indication of the important role that they played. Typically, the mother giving birth may sing,

Mai chilimundaee mai ntulaa!
Mai chilimundaee mai ntulaa! [221]

The midwife would respond by encouraging her to be courageous because not every individual is lucky enough to be in her position,

Ntanginingile mwinyumbi inkulu
Ntanginingile mwinyumbi inkulu
Ntanginingile nene chilombwe! [222]

Following independence in 1961, traditional dances, for example the Kalagwa, Kabhonte, Msakato, and Iyali began to lose significance. This was largely due to the return of migrant workers who had been working on sisal farms in places such as Muheza, Korogwe and Pangani in Tanga region and who brought with them a new and different culture. As noted above, many Pimbwe living in Mpimbwe

---

219. Translated directly, this means "That you have built a strong bridge ... Germans."

220. This means: "We must take our chief to Chala. Don't be tired until you reach Chala."

221. Translation is "Mother, help me, there is something in my stomach."

222. Translation is "I can't enter in to the highness house; I can't enter into the highness house As a midwife I can't enter to the highness house", in which we understand highness being in reference to the expectant mother's belly.

aspired to adopt the new ways of the migrant workers, producing a new cultural mélange, neither entirely Pimbwe nor very far removed from the traditional ways. It is said that those who were not interested in learning about another way of life were perceived as uncouth; they faced problems in finding a lover, because no one wished to pursue a liaison with someone who was not open to new cultural forms of material progress.

Picture 16. Making music with stools on water pots. Photo Monique Borgerhoff Mulder (2008).

Most villages had one or more areas where people, particularly elders, came together to eat, rest and discuss matters after work. This was called an *ibhanja*, and became a vital part of a traditional emphasis on community and sharing. Villagers would attend different *ibhanja* according to the specific zone of the village where they lived, and here they would come every day to chat and share food.[223] It is unclear the extent to which food was communally cooked and shared in Mpimbwe, since there are other reports that every household cooked and prepared their own food which included meat, *madimu*, maize porridge and vegetables such as pumpkin leaves. It is nevertheless clear that at least some of the meat that men hunted in the forest was divided among multiple households for the women to cook collectively at the *ibhanja*. People were expected to behave respectfully and morally whilst at the *ibhanja*. Those who ate their food privately or ate too much were considered to be rude and discourteous, and could be excluded from the *ibhanja* and other sources of help. This morality appears to

---

223. It is said that up to fifteen families would share one *ibhanja*.

have once extended even to the chief, who would often eat at the *ibhanja* with the *Wakuling'anga*, his assistant in providing special medicines. Rumour has it that there was once a chief who allegedly took some of the food and ate it by himself, the impropriety of which resulted in the *Wakuling'anga* and other village administrators attempting, albeit unsuccessfully, to remove him from power.

The *ibhanja* was also venerated as a place where traditions could pass freely from one generation down to another. Young men and children were able to sit watching elders talk, discuss and make speeches, and this proved to be a great public forum for transmitting cultural knowledge. It was in this way that future generations learned from their grandfathers how to become helpful and respected members of society.

Most of what a young man or woman learnt about Pimbwe culture was transmitted at the *ibhanja*; there were no formal general educational institutions in Mpimbwe in traditional times. Socialization of little boys often fell to the grandfather. Whilst it was his responsibility to ensure that his grand-sons were properly prepared for adult life, he did not carry out this role for his grand-daughters. Other very important persons for a growing child were the mother's brother, and also the father's sister. Both provided instruction and ritual support to the younger generation. Daughters spent a great deal of time with their mothers and their mother's sisters, learning about domestic roles. Indeed, it is quite clear that most informal education occurred within the family and the extended family; it was not until the arrival of the Germans and the British that a more formal type of education was introduced.[224] Finally while there was some memory in the 1930s of secret societies for men and women (*malombwe*), possibly related to the Chief Nsumba,[225] there is no remaining memory now.

In a society where there was no reliance on scientific information, it is unsurprising that people relied heavily on signs and premonitions to provide the logic with which to deal with uncertainty, risk and causality. For example, a season of many mangoes signalled a lack of food in the upcoming agricultural cycle, and an outbreak of the disease *upele* (scabies) meant that there would be a disaster in the village such as a drought. The rationale behind this was that the spirits were angry, were giving *upele* as a punishment and were likely to send further punishments. Overall, the Pimbwe were living amidst a world of demanding spirits who could become easily displeased and send vengeance at any time, and it is to their divinities, their ancestral spirits, their diviners, their doctors and their witches that we finally turn.

5.4 Divinities, Spirits and Other Powers

---

224. Oral interview with Baraka Kasimoto (July 2011).

225. Père Maurice (1938), p.95.

The Pimbwe worshipped (and to some extent still do worship) various gods or spirits in order to secure goodwill. The supreme god of the Pimbwe is Ilyuba, identified with the sun and the creator of life and prosperity. The most important tribal divinity is Katavi, who has the ultimate power to control rain and epidemics such as smallpox and measles. In the early days, Pimbwe chiefs were held in such high esteem that if no rain came, their authority was not questioned. However, as their influence has waned from colonial times onwards, any lack of rain has been used as justification that a chief has lost his power. The God Katavi is said to reside in a flood-plain, also called Katavi, in the area now protected for wildlife (discussed below) where he is worshipped beneath a large tree called Wamwelu, named after his wife. The tree is located inside Katavi National Park, some believe within the traditional territory of the Bende. In some stories, his livestock are antelope and he allegedly rides an elephant as a means of transport. In other stories, he herds hippos across the flood plain. It is said that he sometimes transforms himself into a whirlwind (*chimvungwa*), but can also appear as a man dressed in a ragged white cloth along the road from Sumbawanga to Mpanda, or as a stranger in Usevya (as in 1900).[226] In the royal village, there was always a female child who was consecrated as Katavi's wife. When Katavi was publicly worshipped, this girl was anointed with oil and decorated with beads, like a bride. When she was old enough to marry, another girl was appointed in her place.

Katavi's wife, Wamwelu, lives by the cold-water spring in Mirumba village, near the edge of the Fipa escarpment. Her hereditary priest, Yalutindi, also lives there. In the past, women who could not have children went to make offerings to her, promising to name their daughter after her, and Katavi if it was a boy. Wamwelu was gentler than Katavi, and believed to be able to intercede with her husband if he had unleashed an epidemic. Another divinity worshipped by the Pimbwe was Chada. His house is supposedly at the centre of Lake Chada and he herds hippopotamus as his livestock, and wild birds as his chickens. Chada is renowned for having many beautiful wives who are dressed in white. Like Katavi, Chada also had a "wife" at the royal village. When she eventually married, no beating of drums was allowed, it was believed that this would cause her to develop a hernia after giving birth to her first child. Chiefs were apparently also not permitted to visit either the village of Mirumba or Lake Chada, where they would face a barrage of stones if they approached. The relationship between Katavi and Chada is not well understood.

Every Pimbwe village customarily had its own special divinities whom villagers could pray to and make sacrifices at special sacred sites, particularly if the community was experiencing hunger or disease. Village headmen or sub-chiefs (*basengi*) would have informed the tribal chief about any particular problem in order

---

226. Père Maurice (1937), p.291.

to gain permission to make sacrifices to these local deities. Before the ceremony, the *basengi* wrapped himself in a black sheet and placed a snail shell pendant (*impazi*) around his neck, and left for the site. Worship involved giving a traditional offering of beer, flour and meat in small round huts (*msonge*) which were crowned with the white shell of a snail known as an *inyonga*. The headman also would select two black and one white female chickens, and one black male goat to take to the ceremonial site; a great deal more meat would be eaten in the village.[227]

Picture 17. Small altar (msonge) for offerings to spirits.
Photo Monique Borgerhoff Mulder (2006).

Local divinities were very important to Pimbwe, and linked to features of the landscape, where they were believed to reside in or next to some natural object to which the offerings were actually made. For example, the people of Mbede worshipped *Katanda* (a sacred tree), those of Manga worshipped *Ngwilo* (the waterfall on the River Msadya) and *Nanyolwa* (a large stone), those of Mpimbwe

---

227. Oral interview with Daniel Kasike (2011).

Village (now Maji Moto) worshipped *Mbdembu*, *Lukensa* and *Kamina* (different trees), and those of Mamba worshipped *Katete* (a sandy precipice in the nearby escarpment) and *Nikolosa* (another tree). Local deities were much respected; if such respect were not given, people believed they and their families would be cursed with strange diseases.

Picture 18. Traditional altar in Manga. Photo Monique Borgerhoff Mulder (2006).

Special prayers were said relating to the problem that a community was encountering. For example, if there was a disease or epidemic, people would offer a gift to the deity asking for forgiveness for any sins that may have been committed in the hope that their problems would end,

Batata mtupungulizye, izawadi dinu udi twabhaletela
Ndi tulinimakosa utwensu mtusamehe, ndibhamalaya, vivi konse bhalipo
Izawadi odi twabhaletela.[228]

Another prayer focused around the need for rainfall,

Twafa ni ndala, ni imvula oih!
Utwensu chino tukulomba.[229]

If a goat or chicken was used for the sacrifice, it would have its neck partially wrung near a small, round snail-shaped house (*mapelo*). It was then left to die of its own accord in a ritual known as *ukusansala*. If the animal ran and died inside the *mapelo*, this was a positive sign that the prayer has been accepted and better times lay ahead.

Ancestral spirits (*imizimu*) were considered to be a large part of family life.

---

228. This means "Our Fathers, forgive us. We have brought our gift to you. If there are any wrongs or prostitutes in the village, they do exist so please forgive us."

229. The translation is: "We are dying of hunger; what we are asking for is rain."

They were periodically reincarnated within their families and a diviner (*mfumu*) was employed after a baby had been born to find out which previous member of the family's spirit had been reincarnated in the infant. The first new millet and maize of the farming season was always offered to these ancestral spirits. They were worshipped at a small altar (*kiloba*) just inside a family's hut on the left.[230] This altar consisted of a small clay shelf, on which offerings were made of either beer, or flour and water (*ulwanga*), and pieces of cloth made from a certain kind of snail-shell. People felt that they must pay due attention to *imizimu* in order to ensure these were not upset. *Vizwa* on the other hand were evil ancestral spirits associated with causing sterility and fatal illness. Once a diviner had identified a *kizwa*, the bones of the corpse which had given rise to the evil spirit were disinterred, sprinkled with medicine and then burnt.

Diviners (*mfumu*, also *sing'anga*) should not be confused with sorcerers or witches (*mlodi*), nor even with traditional doctors (*sing'anga*). Diviners could identify bad spirits (*vizwa*), excise these, and sometimes even become possessed by spirits.[231] Witches, or sorcerers, harm people directly. They operated at night, by using part of their victim – hair, blood, urine, or even the sand from a footstep. They were greatly feared. They learned from one another, and had to do something cruel to a relative to prove themselves worthy of being a witch.[232]

Traditional doctors (*sing'anga*) had yet a different role, although many of them could also divine sorcery or witchcraft. When somebody's health fails them, they would typically seek treatment from a traditional doctor. Becoming a traditional doctor often runs through the family line and so sons have the opportunity to learn the skill from their father, in some cases paying an "apprenticeship fee".[233] Once they are knowledgeable enough, they go through an initiation ceremony which lasts seven days and typically involves drumming, the use of local brew, meals of goat and chicken meat, and plenty of traditional medicine. On the final evening the drum is beaten continuously throughout the night whilst the man in question sits in a small hut built specially for him. It is his role to cut the neck of both a goat and a chicken directly in front of his *msonge* (places to make offerings to the spirits). If the animals run and die inside the *msonge*, then this is taken as a sign that the preparation is going well for him to become a doctor. If they do not die inside the *msonge*, then the same process is repeated until they do.

230. Willis (1966), p.60.

231. Père Maurice (1938), p.24.

232. Père Maurice (1938), p.269.

233. Oral interview with John Mpepo (July 2011).

The business of treating sick people takes place at the traditional doctor's *msonge*. Here incense is burned, songs are sung and the doctor will listen to the person's symptoms; he will then prescribe what he thinks is the correct treatment. If the pain is physical, such as back pain, stomach pains or broken bones, he will often use both his dreams and the dreams of his patient over the following nights to ensure that exactly the correct treatment is prescribed. This might well involve a mixture containing tree bark (*msawalo* and *mnyinga* are popular trees and saps to use, as is a strong-scented grass known as *kamvumbi*) and the powdered bone of an animal (most likely to be a pangolin known as a *kakakuona*). It may take several dreams over the course of a few nights before exactly the right treatment is given.

If the traditional doctor (*sing'anga*) believes the illness to be caused by witchcraft, i.e., that his patient has been bewitched, then there were several different methods of treatment. For example, if a patient is blind or suffers from some form of fit like epilepsy, then the doctor may put local medicine on the forehead to try to draw out the 'evil' with a stone believed to have magnetic powers. Or they may fill a pot with local medicine and water, heat it up and then cover the sick person's face over it for a few minutes. The thinking behind this is the dirt should come out of the individual and fall into the pot, leading to a complete cleansing. Another method used to treat someone who is spiritually unwell is to take the patient to the forest where he or she is placed in a hole that has been dug in the ground. A special medicine is then poured over her, thereby cleaning her from top to bottom and draining the bad spirit out of her soul. If this is unsuccessful, then the patient may be taken to a nearby river where a preparation from a gourd is poured over her. The principle is the same – the water will wash the sickness away and she will be healed from the injuries inflicted by invasive spirits.

In Mpimbwe tradition there was no belief in an afterlife. The principal fear after death is of becoming a bad spirit, and even this is not thought to be caused by behaviour in life.[234] Beliefs in general divinities, in deities associated with particular locations, in good and bad ancestral spirits, and in the powers of diviners, witches and traditional healers are all ways of making some sense of the life's fates. We have discussed these phenomena in the past tense, but many such beliefs persist, sometimes in altered forms, until today.

---

234. Père Maurice (1937) p.296.

CHAPTER SIX

PIMBWE IN MODERN TIMES

6.1 Independence and Ujamaa

In December 1961, bureaucratic control was consolidated by the British and passed to an independent Tanganyika, which later formed a union with Zanzibar to become Tanzania. In 1962, the Government carried out an administrative reorganization. The Tanganyika Local Government Ordinance (Amendment) Act of February 1962 marked the legal end of indirect rule. This Act also repealed the African Chiefs (Special Powers) Ordinance, and the final step taken to strip chiefs of all their statutory powers was taken in February 1963 when the African Chiefs' Ordinance was itself repealed.[235] Chiefs were from now on given the option of cooperating with the new government or confining themselves to ritual activity.[236]

The years 1973-1976 saw a concerted attempt by the Tanzanian Government to permanently resettle some of the country's population in centralized villages with socialist cooperative agriculture. This villagisation programme was a key feature of the new vision of African socialism and self-reliance (*Ujamaa*). While strangely reminiscent of earlier colonial concentration policies, Tanzania's villagisation programme was the largest forced resettlement scheme undertaken in independent Africa up to that time. It is however fair to say that the policy had none of the ethnic cleansing or military security connotations of South Africa's forced removals or the violent conflicts that have engulfed Rwanda and Burundi. Mwalimu Julius Nyerere, Tanzania's first head of State, instead viewed resettlement as essentially a 'continuum' of the colonial policy agenda and, alongside TANU (Tanzania's official political party), believed it to be the best means possible of delivering social services such as schools, clinics, education and clean drinking water to remote areas like Mpimbwe. He also believed it to be the answer to the development of a more modern, productive agricultural system which, with machinery made available in *ujamaa* villages, would yield a greater marketable surplus especially for export.

As well as his desire to resettle people as part of the national development and welfare project, Nyerere had a more overtly political goal in wanting to, "turn the country away from capitalist development and set it on a different path through creating a nation of *ujamaa* villages (socialist cooperatives)."[237] His ideal system of government was where people would cooperate directly with each other in small

---

235. Willis (1966), p.xv.

236. Waters (2009), p.75.

237. James C. Scott. Seeing Like a State: How Certain Schemes to Improve the Human Condition Failed (2004), p.230.

groups, and where these small groups would then work together to carry out joint enterprises.

Some major advances in literacy and life expectancy were made as a result of *ujamaa* policies, but not in the agricultural sector. Nyerere had complete faith in the role that science played in agriculture, such that he and his administrative teams tended to dismiss the views and knowledge of the farmers themselves. It was against this backdrop that the policy of *ujamaa* resettlement presented itself in such a favourable light to the government – providing the opportunity for the state to take control of farming practice in a new administrative and often geographical environment. Equally, since an estimated eleven out of twelve million rural dwellers lived "scattered" across the landscape at independence (the majority practicing subsistence farming or pastoralism), gathering them into fixed, permanent settlements was a way of asserting greater control over the population and also of preventing tax evasion. Ironically, this logic was similar to that of the earlier resettlement schemes undertaken by both the Germans and particularly, in 1927, by the British.

Nyerere first insisted that the creation of *ujamaa* villages should be gradual and completely voluntary. His opinion was clear: "Socialist communities cannot be established by compulsion. The task of leadership and government is…to explain, encourage and participate."[238] Nyerere believed, in hindsight naïvely, that if a few families were successful in relocating and planting a communal plot of farmland, their success would attract others. However his policy, which has been described by Goran Hyden as a way "to capture the peasantry",[239] was viewed negatively by the ordinary citizen who was not at all keen to move. This was despite incentives such as piped water, schools, health clinics and famine relief being offered to those who did so. Some who went voluntarily tried to ensure that these services were set up before they moved, but this it seems was rare. However, there is no doubt that primary schools and rudimentary western health care services did emerge in many villages during these years.

In 1972, the Government recognized that they needed to restrict the power of local elites if the centralized policies were to be implemented. They therefore abolished the legal autonomy of Village Councils, only retaining the structure in order to implement their development projects. At the same time, regions (as regional provinces) were promoted to the same status as ministries and were provided with their own annual budget, all done in an attempt to ensure that peasants cooperated with government wishes.[240] This also marked the end of

---

238. Scott (2004), p.231.

239. Scott (2004), p230.

240. Hyden, G. Beyond Ujamaa in Tanzania: Underdevelopment and an Uncaptured Peasantry (1980), p. 134–135.

Nyerere's policy of voluntary resettlement. By 1973, the President had gauged the general resistance to villagisation and had developed an "underlying conviction that the peasants did not know what was good for them."[241] In December of that year, the entire machinery of state was therefore put behind compulsory, universal villagisation.[242] The implementation of the 1974 Operation [Planned] Villages was overtly coercive. Nyerere's argument was that he did not want to see his people leading a "life of death" and that the State had to adopt the role of the "father" to ensure a prosperous and improved future.[243] Violence occurred frequently as villagers tried to resist forced resettlement. Both the army and the militia were mobilized to provide transport and to compel compliance, including burning homes to prevent people from returning to their old lands. Some people took what possessions they could and then fled the new village at the earliest opportunity.

The new settlements involved closely packed houses placed in straight lines along the roads, with the fields outside the village organized in block farms. Situating villagers along the roadside may have permitted greater state control over them, but its economic logic was extremely poor from the perspective of the farmer since distances between the houses and the farmland meant that agricultural production suffered greatly. Farmers from that period remember being ordered to work on communal farms rather than their own private ones. National borders were closed to prevent export of products outside of government channels. Some informants in Mpimbwe reported trying to start up small business such as selling salt to make some private money but this proved difficult because of the long journey to Uvinza to get the salt.[244] In imposing this new society from above, Nyerere and his team had failed to comprehend that its success would not just depend on a system that was aesthetically pleasing and bureaucratically manageable. It also had to work for the people who lived there. A captured peasantry does not necessarily result in a productive peasantry if those who are affected by the new system do not like it. Ultimately, the *ujamaa* campaign proved to be a failure economically, and indeed ecologically as soils in the vicinity of the settlements rapid became over-used.

There are a few different reasons for the failure of the cooperative farms, but the key ones revolve around the fact that the state had paid almost no attention to the local and extremely diverse knowledge and practices of cultivators and

---

241. Scott (2004), p.231.

242. Scott (2004), p.234.

243. Coulson, A. Agricultural Policies in Mainland Tanzania. Review of African Political Economy (Winter 1977), p.74.

244. Oral interview with Baraka Kasimoto from Kibaoni village (July 2011).

pastoralists.[245] Firstly, the authorities saw the hinterlands as a static, unchanging solution to a flexible environment in which the farmers had years of experience in honing a strategy to suit the vagaries of rain, wind, heat, pests and wild animals that affected production, on each particular soil type, in each season. For example, by settling farmers in fixed centralized villages, this rendered crop protection and pest control trickier than in the past, and also meant people spent a great deal of time walking to and from their farming plots. Many residents of Mpimbwe report on increased loss of crops to wild animals, pests and also to thieves during the Ujamaa period. Secondly, the planners ignored essential variables such as family size and composition, sideline occupations and gender divisions of labour. For example, the residents of Mpimbwe found that fishing, hunting, and honey collection were more difficult when settled in large villages far from the bush. Thirdly, the state developed a preference for monocropping over the farmers' long established technique of polycropping. Although the environments were often better suited to the latter, the agricultural field officers judged people on whether cash crops were planted in straight, properly spaced rows and mixed with no other crop.

In many parts of Tanzania, including Mpimbwe, the economic situation deteriorated during Ujamaa due to both the state and the peasants acting in self-interest. Officials often exaggerated their achieved goals and predictions to their supervisors in an effort to demonstrate competency and ensure promotion. This made planning difficult because the figures were strongly biased. Nyerere perceived the outcome of the campaign only through the self-congratulatory official reports. At the same time, farmers were hostile to the new regulations and worked on their private holdings instead of the communal lands whenever they could, despite official remonstrance. This again decreased the output of the communal plot, and in fact, agricultural production reached such a low level that large food imports were required from 1973 to 1975.[246] The food shortages (and reliance on imports) became so acute that by 1983 most communal farms were abandoned. Many households regained control of their former fields and began to assert customary rights in both the old plots and the new plots assigned to them at villagisation. In fact, in remote areas like Mpimbwe, many farmers reported having returned to their original homes within only a few years of the forced resettlement.

---

245. Scott (2004), p.225.

246. Scott (2004), p.239. Nyerere in fact declared that the 1.2 billion shillings spent on food imports would have brought one cow for every Tanzanian family.

The Ujamaa campaign had negative political impacts as well, as villagers became critical of the government. Talking of Tanzania as a whole, Scott says,

"far from achieving populist legitimacy, the villagisation campaign created only an alienated, sceptical, demoralised, and uncooperative peasantry for which Tanzania would pay a huge price, both financially and politically."[247]

The extent to which such political alienation occurred in Mpimbwe is unclear, although reports from the majority of those whom we interviewed suggest the price was high. Furthermore, it is worth remembering that similar villagisation programs had failed before in Rukwa, as we saw with the British clearances in 1927. Nevertheless, the Tanzanian state's relatively weak reach into the remote areas of its dominion, together with peasants' options for strategic evasions (including fleeing the villages, unofficial production and trade as well as apathy on the communal land), probably ensured that the practice of Ujamaa was somewhat less destructive than the theory.[248]

Since the mid 1980s, and particularly under the World Bank and International Monetary Fund's Structural Adjustment Programme for Africa, Tanzania has increasingly moved away from the socialist model, adopting more business-friendly neo-liberalist policies and reforms. In places like Rukwa these developments were slow to be felt. Extensive poverty across rural Tanzania, combined with the failing aspirations of African socialism, led to more left-leaning European nations providing large sums of aid to Tanzania. In Rukwa much of this aid came from Norway. Between 1978 and 1996, the Rukwa Integrated Rural Development Project (RUDEP) was supported by the Norwegian government to the tune of about 70 million US dollars (USD), with the catchy campaign *"Rukwa Ruka"* which translates as Rukwa Fly! The central goal was to improve the material well-being of the people, focusing initially in 1978 on a programme to secure safe drinking water to all villages in the region. In its peak years between 1990 and 1994, there were activities in many different sectors including health, education and community development.

Starting in 1992 a project focused on tree planting and primary health was started in Mpimbwe Division by RUDEP. Mpimbwe was chosen on account of both its transport problems and it decreasing agricultural yields – the latter attributed in part to land degradation and escalating conflict between Pimbwe and the more recently arrived Sukuma (see below). The programme in Mpimbwe lasted only two years and its outcome was judged as meagre.[249]

---

247. Scott (2004), p.237.

248. Scott (2004), p.247.

249. Jerve, Alf-Morten and E.J.K. Ntemi. Rukwa Ruka: The Attempt of a Foreign Donor to Uplift a Neglected Region: A Study of the Impact of Norwegian Aid to Rukwa Region, Tanzania. CHR Michelsen Institute (CMI) (2009), p. 73.

6.2 Katavi National Park

The original Pimbwe chiefdom constituted much of what is now the southern part of Katavi National Park in the northern Rukwa Valley. However, gradually the Pimbwe found themselves pushed south, out of their original habitats, in order to make way for the various land protectionist strategies of the colonial era, and later for *ujamaa* villages. As we have already seen, many people were removed from their original villages in 1927 owing to a sleeping sickness epidemic and a colonial desire to create centres for education, commerce and schools. Then in 1956 Katavi was turned into a Game Reserve, and in 1974, it was upgraded to national park status (Katavi National Park) with a surrounding game reserve (Rukwa Game Reserve). This marked an attempt by the Tanzanian Government to turn the Katavi-Rukwa zone into both a conservation area and a source of touristic income for the country. This policy was cemented in 1998 when, with the support of the surviving Konongo chief Nsalamba,[250] the national park was enlarged to the southeast.

The Katavi-Rukwa area is part of the central Zambezi miombo tropical and subtropical woodlands ecoregion.[251] Katavi National Park is now the third largest national park in Tanzania (4471km^2).[252] The principal floodplains of the park are connected by a series of rivers, the main one of which is the Katuma River watershed that lies to the northwest and outside the park. The Katuma flows into the park and feeds Lake Katavi, a floodplain that usually retains some water throughout the dry season. Water drains from Lake Katavi back into the Katuma, which then flows past the Tanzania National Parks (TANAPA) headquarters at Sitalike and into the Katisunga floodplain which is additionally supplied by springs and dry season streams. Water from this floodplain then drains at Ikuu into the Katuma River again. The Katuma flows into Lake Chada, a third floodplain which is additionally fed by the Ngolima River. Lake Chada finally drains into the Kavuu River and leaves the national park eventually flowing into Lake Rukwa. In sum, the three floodplains are mainly supplied and connected by the Katuma River originating outside Katavi National Park. National conservation policies bring great potential to the Rukwa Valley, attracting NGO support, for example the Katavi-Rukwa Conservation Project supported by the German government, but also cause social and economic problems for the local residents of the area in so far as opportunities for hunting and fishing are greatly curtailed.[253]

---

250. Nsalamba was the first MP for Mpanda, and a post-independence community leader.

251. Burgess et al., Terrestrial Ecoregions of Africa and Madagascar: A Conservation Assessment (2004). *Miombo* is the Kiswahili term for the *Brachystegia* genus of tree found in these areas.

252. Katavi-Rukwa Management Plan (2002).

253. Borgerhoff Mulder, M. et al. The Role of Research in Evaluating Conservation Strategies in Tanzania: The Case of the Katavi-Rukwa Ecosystem", Conservation Biology, 21 (2007).

Picture 19. Flooded miombo woodland. Photo Monique Borgerhoff Mulder (2007).

6.3 Contemporary Chiefs

Gradually, chiefly influence waned as British colonialists imposed their will on local societies and undercut chiefly power in order to ensure their own authority was not challenged.

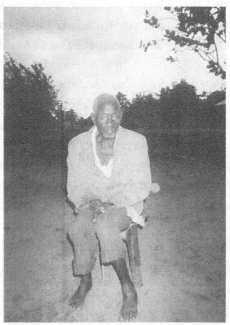

Picture 20. John Kalele Zunda in Muze, aged 81. Photo Peter Mgawe (2009).

The effect of missionaries and their western culture ended the burial practices involving a three-legged stool and the supposed "pillow" rest of two young boys, and other related human sacrifices. Nyerere also worked to ensure a reduction in the chiefs' power consistent with his "modernist" ambitions and democratic principles such that they are nowadays granted much less respect than in the past, in many ways merely representing symbols of a bygone era. Today, there are still two chiefly lines in Mpimbwe, mirroring the conflicts we have seen over the last century. How did these chiefs inherit their positions?

When Chief Kaninsya Bonifasi died, his rightful heir John Kalele Zunda was sidelined and the chieftaincy was instead granted to Thadeo Ngomayalufu II. This greatly angered Kalele who consequently went to live in Muze (outside of the Pimbwe kingdom) near Lake Rukwa. Ngomayalufu II was the sister's son of chief Kasogera and lived in a grass house in Usevya. He was renowned for being a womanizer and, in both 1954 and 1956, the villagers whose wives he had "stolen" burned his house down. As a result, the District Commissioner in Mpanda held a meeting to demand that local people "contribute" to the rebuilding of Ngomayalufu's house. They raised the money and two houses were built – one for the chief and one for his *karani* (secretary). Ngomayalufu lived there until his death in 2003 when he was buried at the Kavuu River.

Picture 21. Chief's house, Usevya. Photo Monique Borgerhoff Mulder (2010).

In 2004, Kalele became chief of Usevya (at age 78) until his death in November 2011. He was unpopular and not well respected as chief, in part because he was physically small. He was a distant sister's son of chief Nsokolo II and was very close to this former chief, learning much about the traditions of chieftaincy from him. Kalele's original appointment by the committee was a divisive move which upset Ngomayalufu's four sons. They began to fight over the chieftainship which was futile because the inheritance always passes through the maternal line to the sister's son. One son in particular, Anando, argued that his father had left all the chieftainship equipment to him when he died, that he was very capable of ruling and that there was no need for Kalele to be chief, particularly since he was absent from the territory. Although Anando's claim to the chieftainship was dropped, he remained in Ngomayalufu's original house until he died, selling off all the chiefly instruments and paraphernalia.[254] Meanwhile, Kalele spent the remainder of his life in Muze, despite efforts by the chiefly administrators to get him back. When a chief dies, it is the duty of the chief's committee to ensure that the body is buried in the territory of Mpimbwe. Indeed, according to tradition, Kalele's body was buried alongside the Kavuu River. There is no certainty that a successor will be chosen.[255] Shortly after his death there were two killings in Usevya, supposedly of relatives of the deceased chief who were believed to be holding back the rainfall. Amongst some members of the chief's council in the northerly section of Mpimbwe there is no will to continue with this institution.

Today's current chief of Mamba is Edes Malaso, otherwise known as Luchensa III. Now aged 82, he is Kalulu's successor and is living in Mamba village. The main stool of the chieftainship which was used by the first Mpimbwe chief (Luchensa) along with the mpazi and other equipment for offerings, are held by this chief. However, he has long claimed that he is not respected as chief of the area and is recognized only in name. In doing so, he provides first-hand confirmation of the demise of chiefly status from bygone days.

---

254. Oral interview with Pigangoma (August 2011).
255. Telephone interview with Pigangoma (September 2012).

Pictures 22. Luchensa III Mamba. Photo Peter Mgawe (2009).

6.4 Where are we Now?

We have already seen that many Pimbwe customs changed both in the pre-colonial period, with the Arab influence, and also in the colonial German and British periods, and how migrant workers returning from sisal plantations in Tabora and other places brought new ideas to Mpimbwe. Independence, the Ujamaa period, and the more recent advance of the global economy have brought many more changes. As authors of this book, we would like to leave readers familiar with Mpimbwe to think about what persists from the traditional realm of the Pimbwe into the 21st century.

The Pimbwe nowadays live in villages where there are members of many of Tanzania's other ethnic communities, most notably Fipa, Nyakyusa, Hutu, Ha, Ndali, Bende, Gongwe and the very numerous Sukuma. So how should one define what it means now to be a Pimbwe? Clearly, as everywhere in Tanzania, Pimbwe children inherit their ethnic identity from their parents and they are marked as members of a particular ethnic group by their mother language. The general belief is that the languages of the Fipa, the Mambwe-Lungu, the Bende, the Rungwa, the Tongwe and perhaps the Urawila are all in the same linguistic cluster as that of the Pimbwe, a situation locals are aware of.[256] The modern Kipimbwe language has changed a lot since pre-colonial times, most likely owing to the intermingling of those languages and migrations of workers to coastal plantations. Kipimbwe also increasingly incorporates Kiswahili words and grammar as a result of trade, settlement and now the national education curriculum. Ethnic groups can be very porous. It is certainly clear that nowadays people tend to "become" Pimbwe as a result of moving into the Rukwa Valley. How true this was of the past is unclear, as is indeed the whole question of exactly where and when the group arose, as we saw with the various Chondo and Luchensa stories.

The fertile flood plains of the Rukwa Valley are also now home to a large Sukuma population. Fleeing poor ecological conditions in the Shinyanga region in the north, the first Sukuma agropastoralists arrived in Mpimbwe in the mid 1970s with their herds of livestock and their strong agricultural traditions. They have also brought their traditional militia organization, the Sungusungu, which plays an important contemporary role in security and policing. To this day the Sukuma continue to arrive, and the two Bantu groups live side-by-side in an area roughly 1200km². The inhabitants of the modern division of Mpimbwe now number almost 90,000, with the Sukuma constituting more than half of this population.[257] The growing influence of the Sukuma has engendered a multi-ethnic and multi-sectorial usage of the valley.[258] There are even some Pimbwe women who marry Sukuma men these days, although fewer marriages occur between Pimbwe men and Sukuma women. There is also some intermingling of the two languages. There is a tendency for Sukuma to pass on their ethnicity more vigorously than the Pimbwe, which means that a child born from parents of mixed ethnicity is inclined to develop a stronger affinity with its Sukuma roots than its Pimbwe ones (although this is not always the case).

As the role of the chief has declined, it has been replaced by elected village chairmen (*mwenye kiti*, Kiswahili) who are responsible for most village affairs, in conjunction with the government appointed executive officer (*mtendaji*, Kiswahili). In some sense, the *mwenye kiti* plays the same role as the elected village headmen (*basengi*) in the past. The ritual offerings made by the *basengi* that were described earlier still persist in some villages. Indeed the importance of local divinities in their sacred sites, and the honouring of these spirits with gifts and ceremonies, remains a central part of the life of more elderly Pimbwe, particularly with respect to controlling rain, sickness and other strikes of fate.

It is clear that most of the Pimbwe's marital traditions and celebrations of the past have gone. However, the more traditional families do engage in certain

---

256. Abe (2011) and Ethnologue (www.ethnologue.com/show_family.asp?subid=75-16) which currently suggests this language family tree.

257. 2012 Population and Housing Census, National Bureau of Statistics, Dar es Salaam (2013).

258. Paciotti, B.C., et al. Grassroots Justice in Tanzania. American Scientist, 93 (2005).

elements of it such as sending a *kikwantemo* to tell the bride's father that someone would like to marry his daughter. Equally, bride price, now normally a cash payment is still paid in many marriages, and some men choose to give hoes and blankets as symbolic gifts, in thanks for the acceptance of their bride price. Nowadays wealth, education and employment are important criteria for choosing a marriage partner, perhaps more so than health. Marriages are also more easily dissolved these days through divorce, since bride price is not consistently paid.[259] Additionally, many young couples live together without a marriage ceremony. All these changes might explain increasing prevalence of the disease HIV-AIDS.

Many of the old Pimbwe songs, music and dances have been forgotten. Some are still retained for use at important ceremonies like weddings and funerals but there is considerabley less emphasis placed upon them. In many cases, they have been replaced by international popular music or the Bongo Flava hip hop styles popular in Dar es Salaam. Whilst the *ibhanja* no longer exists in practice, there is conflicting opinion on whether its influence and values are still retained in some format. Nowadays people sit on their porches (*baraza*, Kiswahili) and, although these are much more private places than the *ibhanja* of the past, they do still provide families with somewhere to eat together and can also act as a forum for discussions amongst visiting friends and relatives. The principle behind the *ibhanja* has therefore perhaps been retained in some way.

With respect to religion, people may still make offerings to Katavi and Wamwelu, but they much more commonly go to church or mosque to ask for help from their God.[260] Today most villages have one or more churches, including Roman Catholic as well as various Protestant and sometimes Christian fundamentalist denominations, although these may be little more than small locally built structures. Muslim communities are also present in many villages, although to date there are only a few mosques. Most individuals seem to combine elements of institutional religions with an awareness of the significance of local deities, ancestral spirits, and their associated ritual practices.

When they get ill, the people of Mpimbwe favour visiting a dispensary or hospital to obtain western medical treatment. However, more persistent medical conditions, particularly if these do not respond well to western medicine, are very often still taken to traditional healers, as is persistent infertility. The drums of the local doctors are still frequently heard throughout the night. This is the case despite growing levels of education, with primary schools now in all villages (but not the more remote sub-villages), and secondary schools in all wards. It seems that the

259. Borgerhoff Mulder, M. Serial Monogamy as Polygyny or Polyandry? Marriage in the Tanzanian Pimbwe. Human Nature 20 (2009).

260. Oral interview with Padre Mwiga (July 2011). Padre Mwiga is preparing a book on the history and development of Christian religion in Mpimbwe.

people of Mpimbwe, like the inhabitants of Europe, America and other developed nations, seek alternative forms of treatment when the standard medical approach does not work. Traditional medicine in Mpimbwe can be cheaper than western medical treatment (although this is not always the case), and has the advantage of being very locally available, so quite commonly it is the first source of help. While most villages now in Mpimbwe have a dispensary, these are neither well equipped nor staffed to deal with serious conditions. Besides, some remarkably successful recoveries occur under the surveillance of traditional doctors.

Witchcraft has not disappeared as an institutional set of beliefs. If an individual is troubled by bad luck, he or she may well suspect a curse; and being cursed can cause unpleasant consequences for the whole family.[261] In fact, increasing wealth inequality may escalate accusations of witchcraft. Families accused of practicing this ancient profession are typically banished to live outside of the village, and cases of suspected witchcraft are sometimes referred to district level court institutions. Mpimbwe is not unique with respect to the prevalence of witchcraft, with accusations of such supernatural meddling occurring in as venerable institutions as the Tanzanian parliament.

Agriculture forms part of the backbone of the Tanzanian economy, and a large number of Pimbwe people depend upon it as their principal source of income, especially since hunting and fishing have become more difficult with the establishment and extension of Katavi National Park. The traditional subsistence crops of millet and cassava are increasingly supplemented by maize (now the principal subsistence crop), and by sunflower, simsim and maize as cash crops. Many families are also adopting a wider variety of vegetable crops (cabbage, onion, tomato) and non-native fruit trees. Use of fertilizer is becoming more common, although only among the richer farmers. Rice cultivation has become a major cash crop on the flood plains adjacent to the rivers. Whilst some of the smaller farmers still follow the storage patterns of the past and use traditional pesticides because these are cheap, others now use modern pesticides which are expensive but are believed to be more effective at warding off insects and vermin. The principal livestock are goats and chickens, and cattle kept largely by the Sukuma but also in varying degrees by other tribes as well. Despite all the energy directed towards food production, food insecurity is still one of the major problems of the people of Rukwa Valley, and particularly the Pimbwe.[262]

261. Borgerhoff Mulder, M. and Beheim, B.A. Understanding the Nature of Wealth and its Effects on Human Fitness. Philosophical Transactions of the Royal Society of London B, 366 (2011).

262. Hadley, C. et al. Seasonal Food Insecurity and Perceived Social Support in Rural Tanzania. Public Health Nutrition, 10, (2007).

With declining levels of water in the rivers, reflecting increases in irrigation and possibly changes in climate, fish are less available in Mpimbwe than they were in the past. Nowadays families buy fish brought by traders from Lake Tanganyika or even Lake Victoria, if they have the spare cash. Regarding game hunting, taboos against hunting animals like zebra and hippopotamus have disappeared, but there has also been a huge decline in the hunting of game animals (with guns, spears and traps) because these species are now formally protected in Katavi National Park, and few are found outside the park borders.

There are still men who go into the national park and game reserve on a fairly regular basis and bring out meat for subsistence and commercial reasons. However, the penalty nowadays is heavy: men caught hunting illegally in the national park may be fined, beaten, or sent to prison in Mpanda or Tabora. Intriguingly the species favoured nowadays (impala, buffalo, warthog, wild pig, giraffe and zebra)[263] are very similar to those that appear in the archaeological excavations in Kibaoni, despite the political, demographic and environmental upheavals of the past two centuries.[264]

Another contemporary issue is the relationship of the Pimbwe with the recently-arrived Sukuma. The Sukuma first came to the area in the 1970s bringing the cattle and plough economy. Their presence has grown since then and a large number of Pimbwe now work, at least seasonally, on Sukuma farms. The increasing prevalence of cattle, and no fencing, can present difficulties because these livestock often invade and trample the Pimbwe fields, destroying harvests and damaging soil through compaction. In bringing larger farms under cultivation than the Pimbwe, the Sukuma are seen by some Pimbwe as monopolizing land as well as causing environmental damage through their extensive clearing of trees. In addition, the bush foods that the Pimbwe fall back on in times of drought are now frequently destroyed by Sukuma cattle.[265] However, the availability of cattle does result in a greater supply of meat and milk being available locally (although the Pimbwe rarely make use of this resource, claiming to dislike the practice of mixing milk from different cows within the same gourd). In addition, the presence of Sukuma (and increasingly Fipa) cattle might also reduce pressure to hunt wild animals for protein, although the price of bushmeat is still lower than that of beef.[266]

263. Martin, A. et al. Bushmeat Consumption in Western Tanzania: A Comparative Analysis from the Same Ecosystem. Tropical Conservation Science 5, (2012).

264. Foutch et al. (2009), p.258. The remains found included a diversity of species such as impala, goats, buffalo, giraffes and perhaps eland. All these are found in Katavi National Park and surrounding areas today & are among the animals commonly hunted by valley inhabitants for both food and profit.

265. Oral interview with Jenita Ponsiano (July 2011). For similar conflicts in the southern part of the Rukwa Valley, see Brockington, D. The Politics and Ethnography of Environmentalisms in Tanzania. African Affairs, 105, (2006).

266. Mgawe, P. et al. Factors Affecting Bushmeat Consumption in Western Tanzania. Tropical Conservation Science 5, (2012).

A rapidly rising population since 1950, an emerging Sukuma agropastoralist community, a low level of education and most critically few economic alternatives to farming and livestock-raising have all significantly contributed to the environmental destruction of the area. Tree cutting, like in many places in Tanzania, is a worrying trend. People need timber for building, baking bricks, and cooking, but as the population in Mpimbwe grows, the pressure on surrounding woodland is unsustainable. Alternative sources of energy are still extremely limited, although a few villages are experimenting with diesel generators that supply the houses of the rich with electricity.

Lion killing is another threat, particularly among the Sukuma where there is a custom of killing a lion when it is threatening, or has indeed attacked, livestock. It also appears that young Sukuma men are increasingly going into the national park to hunt lions, even if these lions constitute no threat to livestock.[267] In addition, Katavi National Park is under threat from both local irrigation schemes to the north that divert water away from the Park, and poaching from Mpimbwe and other areas.[268] Finding a balance between meeting the needs of human communities and the necessity of protecting natural ecosystems is an ongoing challenge in Mpimbwe, as elsewhere in rural Tanzania. The current efforts to implement Wildlife Management Areas, whereby local communities manage land set aside for conservation and reap the economic benefits, may be a step in the right direction.

Some positive signs are that both the Tanzanian government and various NGOs are trying to work with inhabitants of Mpimbwe to conserve their natural environments. Some local people are strongly committed to the conservation of their area, especially their sacred sites at Lakes Chada and Katavi. They feel that Katavi should be embraced and conserved as a landmark for the ancient settlements of Pimbwe. For others though, facing poverty and uncertainty, the placing of natural resources off limits is seen as an unjust affront. The introduction of programmes such as "A Day in the Park", in partnership with Tanzania National Parks, in which school children in Mpimbwe are given an opportunity to visit the national park and learn about the wildlife, ecology and history of the area, will help make the younger generation understand better the need to conserve natural resources, both for the good of people and nature.[269] Some Pimbwe are similarly concerned with protecting the memory of places such as the hot spring

---

267. Fitzherbert, E. et al. From Avengers to Hunters: Leveraging Collection Action for the Conservation of Endangered Lions". Biological Conservation, 174, (2014). See also Genda, P. et al. Launching Watu, Simba na Mazingira project in Katavi-Rukwa. Kakakuona, October-December, (2012).

268. Elisa, M. et al. A Review of the Water Crisis in Tanzania's Protected Areas, with Emphasis on the Katuma River-Lake Rukwa Ecosystem. International Journal of Ecohydrology and Hydrobiology, 10, (2010).

269. Borgerhoff Mulder, M. et al. Children and National Parks. Miombo, (2009).

at Maji Moto and the house where Chief Thadeo Ngomayalufu lived in Usevya. These are all challenges for the future. Meanwhile, considering conservation in a more modern context, it is clear that longer-term solutions lie in diversifying the economy so that people can make a living other than through sole reliance on the land and natural resources. The recently improved access to the national transport network, and the incorporation of Mpimbwe into a new district (Mlele), itself part of a new region (Katavi), will hopefully help to promote new economic ventures in the Rukwa valley.

Picture 23. Offerings (matambiko) at the tree sacred to Katavi on Lake Katavi, made by a mixed group of Pimbwe and Sukuma (August 2012). Photo Peter Genda.

In this final section to the book, we have outlined very briefly how the history and culture of the Pimbwe has shaped the current conditions for the people of Mpimbwe. We hope that our efforts will help to keep the memories of history, identity and sacred places alive in the minds of the people of the Rukwa Valley, whatever their own ancestry. We hope too that we will stimulate the Pimbwe people to remember their culture, and to continue to document how it is changing and adapting to the conditions of the 21st century.

BIBLIOGRAPHY

Abe, Yuko. The Continuum of Languages in West Tanzania Bantu: A Case Study of Gongwe, Bende and Pimbwe. In Geographical Typology and Linguist Areas, edited by O. Hieda, C. König and H. Nakagawa. Amsterdam: John Benjamins Publishing Co., 177-188 (2011)

Andimile, Martin, Caro, Tim and Borgerhoff Mulder, Monique. Bushmeat Consumption in Western Tanzania: A Comparative Analysis from the Same Ecosystem. Tropical Conservation Science, 5, 351-362 (2012)

Borgerhoff Mulder, Monique. Serial Monogamy as Polygyny or Polyandry? Marriage in the Tanzanian Pimbwe. Human Nature, 20, 30-50 (2009)

Borgerhoff Mulder, Monique and Beheim, Brett, A. Understanding the Nature of Wealth and its Effects on Human Fitness. Philosophical Transactions of the Royal Society of London B., 366, 344-356 (2011)

Borgerhoff Mulder, Monique, Caro, Tim, M., Msago, Ayubu Omari. The Role of Research in Evaluating Conservation Strategies in Tanzania: The Case of the Katavi-Rukwa Ecosystem. Conservation Biology, 21, 647-658 (2007)

Borgerhoff Mulder, Monique, Chumo, Caroline and Susuma, Kusekwa. Children and National Parks. Miombo, (2009)

Brockington, Daniel. The Politics and Ethnography of Environmentalisms in Tanzania. African Affairs, 105, 97-116 (2006)

Burgess, N., Hales, J., Underwood, E., Dinerstein, E., Olson, D., Itoua, I., Schipper, J., Ricketts, T. & Newman, K. Terrestrial Ecoregions of Africa and Madagascar: A Conservation Assessment. California: Island Press, World Wildlife Fund (2004)

Coulson, Andrew. Agricultural Policies in Mainland Tanzania. Review of African Political Economy, 4, 74-100 (1977)

Deutsch, Jan-Georg. Emancipation without Abolition in German East Africa, c.1884-1914. Oxford: James Currey (2006)

Elisa, M., J. I. Gara, and E. Wolanski. A Review of the Water Crisis in Tanzania's Protected Areas, with Emphasis on the Katuma River-Lake Rukwa Ecosystem. International Journal of Ecohydrology and Hydrobiology, 10, 1-13 (2010)

Farrant, Leda. Tippu Tip and the East African Slave Trade. London: Hamish Hamilton, (1975)

Fitzherbert, Emily, Borgerhoff Mulder, Monique, Caro, Tim and Macdonald, David W. From Avengers to Hunters: Leveraging Collection Action for the Conservation of Endangered Lions. Biological Conservation., 174, 84-92 (2014)

Foutch, Amy E., Steele, Teresa E. and O'Brien, Christopher J. Faunal Analysis from Kibaoni, a Late Precolonial Pimbwe Village in Rukwa Valley, Tanzania: First Reconstructions of Cultural and Environmental Histories. Azania, 44, 257-267 (2009)

Genda, Peter, Borgerhoff Mulder, Monique, Caro, Tim, Fitzherbert, Emily, and Ballard, Heidi. Launching Watu, Simba na Mazingira Project in Katavi-Rukwa. Kakakuona, October-December, 55-56 (2012)

Hadley, Craig, Borgerhoff Mulder, Monique and Fitzherbert, Emily. Seasonal Food Insecurity and Perceived Social Support in rural Tanzania. Public Health Nutrition, 10, 544-551 (2007)

Hughes, Anthony John. East Africa: Kenya, Tanzania Uganda. London: Penguin Books (1969)

Hyden, Goran, Beyond Ujamaa in Tanzania: Underdevelopment and an Uncaptured Peasantry. Berkeley: University of California Press (1980)

Iliffe, John. A Modern History of Tanganyika. Cambridge: Cambridge University Press (1979)

Jerve, Alf-Morten and Ntemi, E.J.K. Rukwa Ruka: The Attempt of a Foreign Donor to Uplift a Neglected Region: A study of the Impact of Norwegian Aid to Rukwa Region, Tanzania. CHR Michelsen Institute (CMI) (2009)

Katavi-Rukwa Ecosystem Management Plan. United Republic of Tanzania, Ministry of Tourism and Natural Resources, Tanzania National Parks. Unpublished Report (2002)

Kjekshus, Helge. Ecology, Control and Economic Development in East African History: The Case of Tanganyika, 1850-1950. Berkeley: University of California Press (1977)

Koponen, Juhani. People and Production in Late Pre-Colonial Tanzania: History and Structures. Helsinki: Finnish Society of Development Studies (1988)

Lechaptois, Adolphe. Aux Rives du Tanganyika. Maison Carrée, Algiers (1932)

Livingstone, David. The Last Journals of David Livingstone, in Central Africa, from 1865 to his Death. London: J. Murray (1874); reprinted Westport: Greenwood Press (1970)

Martin, Andimile., Caro, Tim and Borgerhoff Mulder, Monique. Bushmeat consumption in western Tanzania: a comparative analysis from the same ecosystem. Tropical Conservation Science 5, 352-364 (2012)

Mgawe, Peter, Borgerhoff Mulder, Monique, Caro, Tim, Martin, Andimile and Kiffner, Christian. Factors Affecting Bushmeat Consumption in the Katavi-Rukwa Ecosystem of Tanzania. Tropical Conservation Science 5, 446-462 (2012)

Oliver, Roland. The Missionary Factor in East Africa. London: Longmans (1952)

Paciotti, Brian, Hadley, Craig, Holmes, Christopher and Borgerhoff Mulder, Monique. Grass-Roots Justice in Tanzania. American Scientist 93, 58-64 (2005)

Père Maurice. Les Pays des Bapimbwe, La Géographie (1935) LXIV, p20, 228,239,309; (1936) LXVI, p171; (1937) LXVII, p86,147,209; (1937) LXVIII, p.224,289; (1938) LXIX, p18,264; LXX, p.83

Scott, James C. Seeing like a State: How Certain Schemes to Improve the Human Condition have Failed. New Haven: Yale University Press (2004)

Smythe, Kathleen, R. Fipa Families. New Hampshire: Heinemann (2006)

Sommerlatte, Malte. Katavi-Rukwa Conservation Project. Bonn, Germany: Kreditanstalt fur Wiederaufbau (1995)

Shorter, Aylward. Chiefship in Western Tanzania. Oxford: Oxford University Press (1972)

Tambila, Anselm. A History of the Rukwa Region (Tanzania) ca. 1870-1940: Aspects of Economic and Social Change from Pre-Colonial to Colonial Times. Ph.D. diss., University of Hamburg (1981)

Thomson, Joseph. To the Central African Lakes and Back, Vol. 2. Boston: Houghton, Mifflin, 1881; reprinted, London: Frank Cass and Company (1968)

United Republic of Tanzania. 2012 Population and Housing Census. National Bureau of Statistics, Ministry of Finance, Dar es Salaam (2013).

Waters, Tony. Social Organisation and Social Status in 19th and 20th Century Rukwa, Tanzania. African Studies Quarterly, 11, 57-93 (2009)

Willis, Roy. The Fipa and Related Peoples of South-West Tanzania and North-East Zambia. London: International African Institute (1966)

Willis, Roy. A State in the Making: Myth, History and Social Transformation in Pre-Colonial Ufipa. Bloomington: Indiana University Press (1981)

Willis, Roy. The Peace Puzzle in Ufipa. In Societies at Peace: Anthropological Perspectives, edited by S. Howell and R. Willis. London: Routledge. 133-135 (1989)

Archival material

Ufipa District Annual Report (1925). Dar es Salaam, Tanzania National Archives

Letter from the Provincial Commissioner, Kigoma Province to The Honourable Chief Secretary, Dar es Salaam, 1st August 1922